Science for Girls?

Science for Girls?

edited by

Alison Kelly

Open University Press
Milton Keynes · Philadelphia

Open University Press
Open University Educational Enterprises Limited
12 Cofferidge Close
Stony Stratford
Milton Keynes MK11 1BY, England

and
242 Cherry Street
Philadelphia, PA 19106, USA

First published 1987

British Library Cataloguing in Publication Data

Science for girls.
  1. Science—Study and teaching
  (Secondary)—Great Britain 2. Education
  of women—Great Britain
  I. Kelly, Alison, *1947–*
  507′.1241   Q183.4.G7

  ISBN 0 335 10295 6

  ISBN 0 335 10294 8 Pbk

Library of Congress Cataloging in Publication Data
Science for girls.

  Includes index.
  1. Science—study and teaching.   2. Women—
Education.   I. Kelly, Alison.
  Q181.S374 1987   500   87–5774

  ISBN 0–335–10295–6
  ISBN 0–335–10294–8 (pbk.)

Text design by Clarke Williams

Typeset by Quadra Associates Ltd, Oxford
Printed in Great Britain by Biddles Ltd, Guildford
and King's Lynn

Contents

PART III Curriculum Content

PART IV Intervention Programmes

     Alison Kelly, Judith Whyte and Barbara Smail
12 Encouraging girls to give physics a second chance   113
     Barbara Smail
13 Increasing the participation and achievement of girls and women   119
     in mathematics, science and engineering
     *Elizabeth K. Stage, Nancy Kreinberg, Jacquelynne Eccles (Parsons) and
     Joanne Rossi Becker*

     Name Index   135

     Subject Index   139

Contributors

Joanne Rossi Becker is Associate Professor of Mathematics at San Jose State University, USA, where she teaches preservice and inservice teachers of mathematics and conducts research on sex related differences in mathematics performance.

Di Bentley has taught in comprehensive schools in the areas of science and health education for twelve years. She has researched the attitudes of girls to science education and youngsters' constructions of teachers' non-verbal communication. She spent three years in curriculum development with the Secondary Science Curriculum Review and is currently employed by the Inner London Education Authority (ILEA) as one of the new Inspectors Based in Schools (IBIS) team.

Margaret Crossman graduated in physics from Manchester University in 1972. She taught physics to A level in a comprehensive school for over six years. She then produced a daughter, an M.Ed. dissertation and a son in less than two years. After part-time posts in various schools she is now teaching part-time in a girls' school.

Jacquelynne Eccles (Parsons) is Professor of Psychology at the University of Michigan, Ann Arbor, USA, where she conducts research on motivation, specializing in sex-related differences in motivation and achievement in mathematics.

Jan Harding has worked in teacher education for a number of years, most recently as Head of the Chemistry Section at the Centre for Science and Mathematics Education, Chelsea College, University of London. She has researched and published in the field of gender and science and technology since the early 1970s and was co-founder of the international Girls and Science and Technology (GASAT) conferences.

John Head lectures at the Centre for Educational Studies, King's College, London. A former school science teacher, Dr Head was a team leader of the Science Teacher Education Project and General Editor of the Nuffield Science 11 to 13 materials. His interest in psychology applied to science education is shown in his book *The Personal Response to Science*.

Alison Kelly took a degree in physics and spent two years teaching maths and physics in a secondary school. She then switched into educational research, and now lectures in sociology at the University of Manchester. Most of her research has been on gender differences in education, particularly in physical science. She has written extensively on this topic, and was co-director (with Judith Whyte) of the Girls Into Science and Technology (GIST) project.

Nancy Kreinberg is Director of EQUALS, Lawrence Hall of Science, University of California, Berkeley, USA. EQUALS is a collection of programmes for staff development, curriculum improvement and parent involvement aimed at increasing the participation and achievement of under-represented students in mathematics.

Barbara Smail graduated in chemistry from the University of Manchester. She has worked in industry in Britain and the United States, and spent several years teaching science to girls in a comprehensive school. From 1979–83 she was Research Fellow/Schools Liaison Officer for the Girls Into Science and Technology (GIST) project. Currently she holds the post of Education Manager for the British Association for the Advancement of Science (BAAS).

Margaret Spear taught chemistry and biology for some years in a wide variety of schools, both in England and abroad. More recently she was at the Open University where she researched into science teachers' attitudes and expectations. Having obtained a PhD she is now a Research Fellow in the School of Education at Reading University.

Elizabeth K. Stage is Director of Math and Computer Education, Lawrence Hall of Science, University of California, Berkeley, USA, where she plans and evaluates inservice programmes for teachers to increase their use of materials, including technology, that promote the success of all students in mathematics.

Michael Sutoris has a first degree in Applied Physics and Social Sciences and a Masters degree in Social and Psychological Aspects of Science and Technology. His research has sought links between psychodynamic processes and gender with specific reference to science choice. He has worked both in industry and in education and is currently teaching science in a North London comprehensive school.

Valerie Walkerdine is a lecturer at the University of London, Institute of Education, where she is also director of the Girls and Mathematics Unit. She trained as a developmental psychologist and since then has attempted to develop feminist work in the area of girls' education and socialization. She has published several books, including *The Mastery of Reason* and *Girls and Mathematics: New Thoughts on an Old Question*.

Mike Watts has taught science for eight years in schools in London and Jamaica. He has researched youngsters' conceptualizations of science at the University of Surrey and undertaken curriculum development with the Secondary Science Curriculum Review. He is currently developing a new post-graduate Certificate of Education course at Roehampton Institute of Higher Education.

Judith Byrne Whyte is a Senior Lecturer at Manchester Polytechnic and is also associated with Manchester Business School. She has published *Beyond the Wendy House* about sex stereotyping in the primary school, *Girls Into Science and Technology: the Story of a Project*, and edited *Girl Friendly Schooling*. Her current research interests include management of education, managerial promotion systems, performance appraisal and equal opportunity personnel policies in the public and private sectors.

Introduction

Alison Kelly

Six years ago I edited a book called *The Missing Half* which looked at the question of girls and science education. At the time this was a very new area of interest. Nothing much had been published on the topic. To get the articles for the book I had to write round to friends and acquaintances who I knew were interested, and ask them to put their thoughts on paper, or to re-examine their existing data to highlight the girls-and-science angle.

It is no exaggeration to say that since then there has been an explosion of interest. In 1981 the first international Girls and Science and Technology (GASAT) conference met with 27 participants from eight Western countries. In 1985 the third conference had more than 100 participants from 20 countries, covering the First, Second and Third World on five continents. Only South America was not represented. The fourth conference, in 1987, is planned to be even bigger.

The changes in research on girls and science over the past few years are not confined to an expansion of interest. There has also been a marked shift in the type of research being carried out. In *The Missing Half* most of us approached the topic from a broadly psychologistic angle. We wanted to know why girls avoided physical science, and we looked for the answer in individual attitudes and personality traits, based on survey methods. This type of work is still popular, and certainly has much to offer. But it has a tendency to blame the victim. Crudely put, the psychologistic approach says that if girls don't do science, there must be something wrong with their perceptions of science, of the world or of themselves. The corollary of this is that intervention strategies are designed to boost girls' confidence, and to correct their misconceptions about science. Girls are expected to change to accommodate science. The hidden message is 'get yourself sorted out and you'll be able to do science'.

The alternative approach which has developed recently is more sociological and structural. It locates the fault at least partially within science, within schools or within society at large. These institutions must change to accommodate girls. Science is not an immutable 'thing'; it is a socially constructed process, which is produced in schools and laboratories in accordance with societal norms. The same is true of girls' subject choices – they do not arise in a vacuum, dependent only on the individual girl's characteristics. Rather they are the end result of a process which involves ideas about masculinity and femininity, and the sexual division of labour (both mental and manual).

Based on this type of thinking, a number of researchers have begun to study the historical construction of science as we know it today, to observe the processes taking place in classrooms, and to analyse curricula. Equally important, we have begun to explore the possibilities for action to remedy the situation. The present collection of articles is intended to reflect these new trends in thinking about girls and science education.

This time I didn't have to write round to friends, asking them to contribute. All the papers already existed; many have been published before. But they were scattered across a variety of journals and conference proceedings, which were not always easy to locate. By bringing the articles together in one volume I hope that the underlying unity of approach will become evident and that they will be more readily accessible to an audience of students and academics in the fields of education, sociology, philosophy and women's studies.

I would also like to think that the book will be read and pondered by concerned science teachers. My own training in physics tells me that the way of thinking embodied in some of the papers, particularly the more philosophical ones, is alien to many scientists. Moreover the language is often difficult (at least for me!) However, the ideas do repay careful study, and I trust they will not be rejected out of hand.

Part I of the collection contains four chapters which propose different – although sometimes interlocking – explanations for girls' problematic relation-ship with school science. The first chapter is a reprint of an article I wrote shortly after *The Missing Half* was published. It outlines some of the conclusions of that book, and indicates to a certain extent the departure point for the new approaches to girls and science. In the article I propose three main reasons for girls' avoidance of science. Girls see science as a difficult subject, and have less confidence than boys in their own abilities; they see science as masculine, which conflicts with their developing sense of femininity; and they see science as impersonal, whereas their socialization has primarily been towards concern for people. While I certainly do not want to disown these ideas, if I were writing the article today it would have a slightly different slant. I would put more emphasis on the role of schools and teachers in dissuading girls from science, and less on girls' internal states. The article suggests that it is necessary to change the *image* of science; I now think that it is necessary to change *science*.

The next two chapters, by John Head and by Jan Harding and Michael Sutoris, both derive from work undertaken at the Centre for Science Education at Chelsea College, and both propose psychological/development type theories. John Head links subject choice to ego-development. He argues that adolescents go through a process of crisis (intensive questioning) and commitment (firm belief) on the way to achieving ego-identity. Science is a conventional and acceptable career choice for boys; moreover it appears to offer clear and firm answers. It is therefore attractive to a considerable number of immature boys who have not yet begun to question conventional wisdom and achieve their own identity. Girls at a similar stage of development tend to avoid science because it is not a conventional choice. Girls who *do* choose science are likely to be more emotionally mature, and to have considerable self-knowledge which helps them to sustain unusual choices.

Jan Harding and Michael Sutoris locate the roots of girls' avoidance of science further back in time. They use object-relations theory to analyse the psychological development of male and female infants. The primary caretaker (usually the infant's mother) has to tread a narrow line between withdrawing her care too soon, demanding too much independence from the infant, and continuing her protection too long. According to object-relations theory, too early a withdrawal of care can lead to separation-anxiety, an attachment to objects and a search for security. In our society this happens more often to boys than to girls, and may lead boys to prefer the certainty of science to the fluidity of the arts. On the other hand too much protection can lead to merging-anxiety, with delayed autonomy and continuing dependence, and this is more characteristic of girls in Western society.

The chapters by Harding and Sutoris and by Head both stress that school science needs to change to make it fit better with girls' development. This is not just in order to encourage more girls into science, but for the health of science itself. A subject which attracts mainly emotionally immature, insecure individuals certainly has problems! I am not entirely convinced that this is an accurate characterization of science and scientsts. But it has at least a grain of truth, and the suggestions these authors make for changing school science are echoed over and over again in this book by writers who approach the topic from many different perspectives.

In the last paper in this section Valerie Walkerdine questions the nature of the 'facts' we know about girls and mathematics, and examines the way in which our conceptions of masculinity and femininity were historically constructed. This is one of the most difficult chapters in the book. It uses ideas from Foucault to argue that, from the seventeenth century onwards, reason came to be located first in the body and then in the mind of men, and that women were axiomatically excluded from reason. Although the argument is made with reference to mathematics, it applies equally well to science.

The second part of the book turns from these theoretical speculations to a consideration of what actually goes on in schools and classrooms. As Margaret Spear points out, surprisingly little research has considered teachers' opinions about girls and boys in science; yet it is commonly asserted that teachers are a crucial influence on children's learning. Spear's two short papers neatly demonstrate some disturbing facts about science teachers. They award higher marks, on average, to work they think is from a boy than to identical work that they think has been produced by a girl; and they consider it more important for boys than for girls to get qualifications in science.

Further disturbing facts about science teachers are revealed in Margaret Crossman's chapter. She shows that teachers interact more with boys than with girls in science lessons. This is true both in physics and in biology lessons, and with both male and female teachers. The imbalance is present in both pupil talk and teacher talk, and although it is most marked in teacher criticism of boys it is also present in other forms of classroom conversation.

The nature of classroom interactions in science is explored in a rather different way in my paper on the masculinity of science. Crossman used a structured observation schedule to quantify the sex differences in teacher-pupil talk. By contrast I used ethnographic methods to describe the sorts of assumptions and behaviours that girls and boys bring with them to school, and the ways in which these are transformed in the laboratory so that science comes to be seen as a male subject. Teachers are (or should be) in control in the classroom, but the children's influence cannot be discounted.

The third part of the book contains two chapters of curriculum analysis. This section is shorter than the others not because it is less important, but because less has been done in this area. Although many authors have suggested that science should be changed in accord with girls' interests, few have spelt out how this is to be accomplished. One writer who has done this is Barbara Smail, who developed the idea of girl-friendly science into a series of work-sheets. The extract from her work which is reprinted here examines some of the principles on which such a girl-friendly science curriculum might be based.

In the following chapter Di Bentley and Mike Watts argue that girl-friendly science represents merely a superficial change in a fundamentally patriarchal subject. They distinguish between girl-friendly science, which changes the packaging of science to make it more attractive to girls; feminine science which demands a change in the classroom environment to place more value on caring and co-operation; and feminist science which would involve valuing science as personal development, adopting a more subjective and holistic approach to nature, and not privileging science over other forms of knowledge. They suggest some of the implications of this for science education. However, I think it is fair to say that the practical details of this approach have yet to be worked out.

The final section of the book discusses some of the intervention programmes which have been implemented over the past few years to try and encourage more girls to continue with the study of science and related subjects. In the first chapter I and my colleagues, Judith Whyte and Barbara Smail, describe the Girls Into Science and Technology (GIST) project. GIST was an action-research project which aimed to explore the reasons for girls' under-achievement in science, and simultaneously to take steps to remedy the situation. We followed a cohort of children in ten comprehensive schools from the time they entered secondary school until they made their option choices three years later. During this time we collaborated with the teachers in the schools to devise and implement strategies designed to encourage more girls to continue with science when it became optional. Some of the research results of the project have formed the basis of earlier chapters in the book. In this chapter we describe the interventions and their effects on the children and teachers with whom we worked. The results are far from clear-cut, but it appears that we were more successful in changing children's ideas of what was *permissable* for girls and boys to do, than in changing their actual behaviour. This can be seen as a hopeful first step. However, the greatest effect of the project may have been in making teachers around the country aware of girls and science as an educational issue with which they should be concerned.

A rather less ambitious intervention is described in the next chapter by Barbara Smail. Precisely because it was less ambitious it was also easier to evaluate. Three university physics departments put on three-day residential courses for girls who had taken O level physics but were doubtful about taking the subject further. Since the courses were over-subscribed a control group of girls who had wanted to come but could not be accommodated was available. Comparisons of these two groups with the national figures for the proportion of girls who continued with the subject after taking O level physics showed that the courses were successful in persuading a considerable number of 'doubtful' girls to persist with physics.

In the final chapter a group of four American writers (Elizabeth Stage, Nancy Kreinberg, Jacquelynne Eccles and Joanne Becker) describe a number of intervention projects which have been tried in the United States. Their education system is of course different from ours, principally in the postpone-ment of major choices to a much later age, the possibility of dropping mathematics before you have had a chance to study physics or chemistry, and the smaller amount of practical work involved in science lessons. These differences are reflected in the interventions they describe, which concentrate on college-age students, and which have a major focus on mathematics and on providing students with 'hands-on' experiences. It is also noticeable that there is far less questioning of the nature of science or of teacher-pupil interactions in the American work than in recent British writing. Nevertheless this paper is interesting because it demonstrates the widespread nature of concern and intervention. In addition it makes it very clear that interventions can succeed in increasing the proportion of women studying science.

Many of the American interventions programmes have been sponsored by the National Science Foundation. In Britain too, official bodies have been concerned with girls' under-representation in science and with attempts to remedy it. The Department of Education and Science undertook an investiga-tion in 1978 (DES, 1980). A few years later they stated that

> The science education of many girls is at present inadequte . . . The aim of every school should be to provide genuine equality of opportunity . . . Particular attention should be given to the expectations and attitudes of girls when reaching decisions on style and methods of teaching, on curriculum content and on time-tabling arrangements (DES, 1985)

The Secondary Science Curriculum Review (SSCR) also insisted that

> whilst all developmental work must be directed towards the needs of pupils of all abilities, detailed attention should be given to the particular aspirations of girls . . . (West, 1982)

Similar statements emanate from the Manpower Services Commission (MSC) in connection with the Youth Training Scheme (YTS) and Technical and Vocational Education Initiative (TVEI) (MSC, 1983; 1984). The Equal Opportunities Commission and the Engineering Council designated 1984 as Women In Science and Engineering (WISE) Year and a busy programme of speakers and visits was organized during the year (EOC, 1984).

It is difficult to know how effective such statements and the attendant publicity are. Certainly the situation is not static. Figure 1 shows the number of pupils who have achieved CSE or O level passes in science subjects, expressed as a percentage of school leavers in England and Wales, over the last 20 years. It is evident that the percentages have all risen, in accord with the general growth in certification. But some have grown more dramatically than others. The figures are subject to all sorts of uncertainties – such as pupils double-entering both CSE and O level examinations, and some O levels being taken after leaving school – but the basic trend is probably accurate. The two largest groups in 1966 – girls in biology and boys in physics – grew steadily, until by 1985 both constituted about 50 per cent of the age group. The two smallest groups – girls in physics and girls in chemistry – grew only slightly until the late 1970s, but have accelerated since then. It is noticeable that the number of girls achieving qualifications in physics and in chemistry was similar in 1966, but that girls' passes in chemistry have grown much faster than girls' passes in physics.

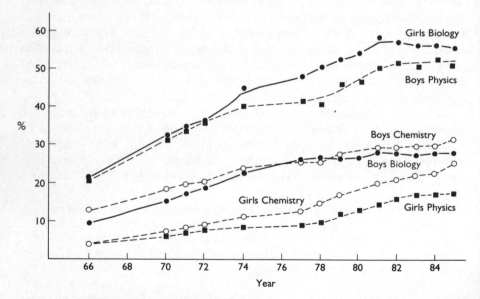

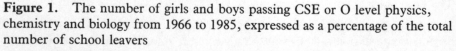

Figure 1. The number of girls and boys passing CSE or O level physics, chemistry and biology from 1966 to 1985, expressed as a percentage of the total number of school leavers

Source: Department of Education and Science *Statistics of Education.*

Table 1. Girls' and boys' representation in CSE and O level physics passes in 1966 and 1984

(a) The number of passes by boys for every pass by a girl			
	CSE	O level	Total
1966	16.8	4.7	6.2
1985	3.3	2.4	2.9

(b) The gap in percentage points between boys and girls			
	CSE	O level	Total
1966	6.3	10.8	17.1
1985	20.3	11.9	32.2

Chemistry is now the science subject which shows the least sex differentiation in certification rates. Boys' passes in biology increased quite steeply between 1966 and 1976, but have levelled off since then, whereas boys' passes in chemistry have shown a slight, steady rise throughout the period.

These figures suggest that the problem of girls and science is really a problem of girls and physics. The gap between the sexes in chemistry seems to be closing, while girls have always been over-represented in biology. The proportion of pupils studying physics until at least the school-leaving age has increased steadily between 1966 and 1986. For boys the figure now hovers around 50 per cent, while for girls it has reached 17 per cent. Whether physics has become more or less male dominated over this 20-year period is an interesting question. Table 1a shows that in 1966 six boys gained a qualification in physics for every one girl; by 1985 the ratio had fallen to three to one. However, Table 1b shows that over the same period the percentage gap between boys' and girls' passes almost doubled. As they say, you can prove anything with statistics!

So far I have assumed that girls' under-representation in physical science is a problem, and that it would be a good thing if more girls could be encouraged to take these subjects when they become optional. But this is by no means self-evident. Some people (including some feminists) argue that science, as taught today, is a dehumanizing activity, and that girls benefit from choosing arts subjects, which allow for greater personal growth. Others suggest that society needs diversity, with a clear distinction between male and female, and that efforts to reduce sex differentiation are misguided. As Cowell (1981) puts it

> feminists, in trying to press girls into [technological] subjects, often against their natural inclinations, are merely helping to propel our civilization down the slippery slope into a completely materialistic way of life.

I do not accept these arguments. But I do accept that the case for encouraging girls into physical science needs to be argued. This can be done in several distinct ways. The first is to stress the restrictions which sex stereotypes place on individuals. If children's choices are limited by what they themselves consider to be suitable for girls or boys, or what their teachers, parents, peers or employers consider to be suitable, then they are not able to develop their potential to the full. Stereotyping reduces liberty. Both the individuals concerned and the society as a whole lose from the restriction of talent.

This argument applies to all sex stereotyping, including that which keeps boys out of subjects like French, biology and home economics. But there are additional reasons why girls' under-involvement in science is of particular concern. These have to do with power and influence in society. Science qualifications help individuals to get jobs – often well-paid secure jobs – in a way that other subjects do not. This is true at all levels from the school leaver with CSEs in physics and technical drawing who is eligible for a range of technical YTS courses, to the graduate scientist or engineer whose employment prospects and starting salary eclipse those of her/his counterpart in arts or social science. There may be jobs for temps in London offices, but their earnings will never match those of car mechanics throughout the country; we may need more social workers, but the papers are full of vacancies for computer programmers.

Not everyone who studies science at school will use their qualifications in their working life. Science is also important as a part of general education, and here too girls are disadvantaged by their exclusion from physical science. We live in a technological society. Science education can give people a sense of control over their environment, rather than being at the mercy of the technology with which they are surrounded. I do not mean by this that everyone should be able to fix their own car or vacuum cleaner when it breaks down. But I do think that everyone should have a sense of what is fixable, and whether it is a major or a minor repair. We should not be scared, as many women are today, of lifting the bonnet of the car or tipping the vacuum cleaner upside down to see what is wrong. Science education can provide the confidence that machinery works in comprehensible ways, which is necessary for this feeling of control.

The arguments about jobs and about our technological environment can both be extended from the individual to the group level. Technology is a powerful force, and at present it is controlled by men. As a feminist I find that disturbing. Women as a group need to be educated in science so that our voices can be heard in technological discussions. Women should be involved in science and technology planning, and women should take an informed part in debates about topics such as telecommunications or the future of nuclear power. Involvement is a more positive strategy than withdrawal for the humanization of science. Women, whose socialization traditionally emphasizes people, are well placed to re-orientate science towards caring concerns.

Research on girls and science education has changed considerably over the past five years. Will the changes continue into the future? Undoubtedly science education itself will change rapidly in the next few years. The SSCR is widely expected to herald the introduction of physical science and biological science for everyone up to school-leaving age. This in itself will, in my opinion, be beneficial for girls, as it will prevent them from cutting themselves off from physical science at the age of fourteen. A couple more years before choices are made means not only a couple more years of science education – and therefore presumably greater knowledge and understanding – but a couple more years of maturity, and a greater likelihood of making choices in the light of their own self-knowledge rather than sex stereotypes.

Many of the authors in this book are calling for more wide-ranging changes in science education than the simple reduction of choice. Some are demanding the total replacement of science as we know it today, while others insist that at the very least science and science teachers must become more socially aware and sensitive to the needs of their female pupils. Unfortunately I am not optimistic about the likelihood of change in these respects.

None of the papers in this volume have touched on issues of power. The political-economy perspective is totally lacking. This is not because I have chosen to exclude papers of this type, but because I do not know of any work on girls and science education in this tradition. In *The Missing Half* there was one article (Saraga & Griffiths, 1981), which attempted to examine the links between capitalism, patriarchy and the exclusion of girls from science. Their work was only exploratory, and it does not seem to have had any descendants.

I think this is a serious omission. Without some understanding of the vested interests which support the status quo, we are unlikely to make much progress in bringing about change. It is noticeable that the chapter which makes the strongest plea for a complete transformation of school science was written by Di Bentley and Mike Watts while they were employed by the SSCR. But it is equally noticeable that their ideas have had not the slightest impact on curriculum materials produced by the Review. Even the Review publication on sex differences takes only very small steps in the direction of the 'girl-friendly' science that Bentley and Watts disdain (Ditchfield & Scott, 1987).

This does not seem to me to be surprising. Change rarely comes about simply because somebody writes a striking article. We urgently need an understanding of the process of change, and the factors which promote or inhibit it. Our experience on the GIST project was that it was all too easy to fall between the Scylla of appearing unacceptably radical, so that our ideas could be dismissed as cranky, and the Charybdis of requesting such small changes that their impact was lost (Kelly, 1985). The best route forward may well be through the 'ripple effect' – making teachers aware that there is a problem, that as professionals they should be concerned about it, and that someone, somewhere has good ideas on what to do. But it is a long, slow process.

Nor is this necessarily a bad thing. Suppose, just for the sake of argument, that a number of enlightened teachers suddenly started teaching feminist science. They value the children's subjective experience, and they teach in an intuitive, holistic way, not a rule-bound atomistic one. Other, more conventional teachers of course continue with the traditional, patriarchal science. Which set of pupils is going to get the examination passes and the jobs? Which, come to that, is going to have the knowledge to build bridges and develop drugs? We must be careful not to throw the baby out with the bath-water.

Without an understanding of power and the process of change there is a real danger of disadvantaging the very people that we mean to help. Many of the most conventional science teachers, those least likely to be attracted by a feminist science, are to be found in independent boys' schools, teaching white, middle class males. If science for them remains unaltered, while science changes for the mainly working class pupils in comprehensive schools, then the latter group are likely to leave school even less able to compete on equal terms than at present.

This then is the area of work that I hope will develop over the next few years. I would like to see a political analysis of the process of change in science education. This should take into account not just sex differences, but also class and race differences. It is noticeable that throughout this volume there has been no mention of socio-economic or ethnic divisions. We have assumed that all girls are similar and all boys are similar. But of course they are not. What is attractive to a white, middle class girl in Esher may be totally irrelevant to a black working class girl in Oldham. These analyses need to made both theoretically and empirically. Links can be forged between girl-friendly science and the developing anti-racist and multi-cultural approaches to science; they can be made by examining attitudes and aspirations in different ethnic and socio-economic groups; they can be explored in classroom interactions and in teacher's opinions. But above all they must be grounded in a consideration of where we are now, and what is possible, starting with the teachers and schools that we have today. Planning the route is as important as knowing the destination.

References

Cowell, B. (1981) 'Mixed and single sex grouping in secondary schools'. *Oxford Review of Education*, Vol. 7, pp. 165–72.

Department of Education and Science (1980) *Girls and Science*, HMI Series, Matters for Discussion, No. 13, HMSO.

Department of Education and Science and the Welsh Office (1985) *Science 5–16: A Statement of Policy*. HMSO. Reprinted in *Education in Science*, No. 112, pp. 21–36, April.

Ditchfield, C. and Scott, L. (1987) *Better Science for Girls and Boys*. Heinemann.

Equal Opportunities Commission (1984) *What is WISE year all about?* EOC, Manchester.

Kelly, A. (ed.) (1981) *The Missing Half: Girls and Science Education*. Manchester University Press.

Kelly, A. (1985). 'Changing schools and changing society'. In Arnot, M. (ed.), *Race and Gender: Equal Opportunities Policies in Education*. Pergamon Press.

Manpower Services Commission (1983) *They're Making the Choice*. MSC, Sheffield.

Manpower Services Commission (1984) *TVEI: Annual Review, 1984*. MSC, Sheffield.

Saraga, E. and Griffiths, D. (1981) 'Biological inevitabilities or political choices? The future for girls in science'. In Kelly, A. (ed.), *The Mising Half: Girls and Science Education*. Manchester University Press.

West R.W. (1982) 'The secondary science curriculum review' *Education in Science*, No. 99, pp. 29–31, September.

Part I
Explanations

1 Why girls don't do science

Alison Kelly

I have always associated chemistry and physics with boys and I have always associated biology with girls. So when I thought of chemistry I thought well boys mostly, so I just scored it out. I don't see why a girl shouldn't be able to do chemistry and physics. I'd like to have done them although I really wouldn't have been very good at them. I'd like to have carried on with them but as I said before, boys' subjects, so I just dropped them.

I chose biology because it seemed to cover more areas of life whereas in chemistry and physics it seemed to be only pouring liquids, powders and gases into test tubes which didn't really appeal to me. Biology I thought . . . could be of help to me in the future . . . But I could not understand much reason to know whether one liquid was heavier than the other etc.

The reasons these girls gave for dropping physical science at school are both disturbing and revealing. Like most girls they had an apparently free choice. Like most girls they decided against physics and chemistry. The question is, why? Three main reasons are implicit in the girls' comments. First, comes lack of self-confidence and the fear that science is too difficult ('I really wouldn't have been very good at them'). Then there is the masculine image of physical science ('I have always associated chemistry and physics with boys'). And third, the apparent remoteness of science from girls' everyday concerns ('I could not understand much reason to know whether one liquid was heavier than another').

Before discussing these reasons in more detail, I want to look briefly at a fourth explanation. It is frequently suggested that there is some biological difference between the sexes which pre-disposes boys to opt for science subjects and girls for arts (see, for example, Gray, 1981). A difference in spatial ability is supposed to be behind this. Scientists generally score higher than non-scientists on tests of spatial ability, and there is a well-established sex difference on these tests, with boys scoring higher than girls. During the 1970s it was widely held that spatial ability was partly inherited via an X-linked recessive gene, and was therefore manifest more often in males than in females. More recent data have cast doubt on this hypothesis, although that does not disprove all biological explanations.

Source: New Scientist, the weekly review of Science and Technology, London, 20 May 1982

However, biological factors cannot be the complete answer. In other countries, particularly in Eastern Europe, large numbers of women study science successfully, despite any biological handicap (see Kelly, 1976). Nor are biological predispositions necessarily relevant when formulating education policy. Girls usually score better than boys on verbal tests, and boys have more difficulty than girls in learning to read. But schools do not take this as a reason for letting boys drop out of reading classes. Quite the reverse: most schools have remedial reading classes which are used predominantly by boys. Teachers put extra effort into teaching boys to read to make up for any deficiency, whether its origin is biological or social. The same could be done to boost the spatial ability of girls if the problems were considered equally serious.

But I doubt whether sex differences in spatial ability lie at the root of the problem. They are just as likely to be a symptom. Children who play with construction toys and handle tools probably develop both their spatial ability and their scientific aptitude in the process. And conventions of child rearing today ensure that such toys and tools are much more frequently made available to boys than to girls.

The way children are reared is also important in developing children's self-image. In our society masculinity is associated with independence, self-reliance, strength and leadership. Femininity is associated with conformity, passivity, nurturance and concern for people. Children are taught and teach themselves and their peers to behave in ways that are appropriate to their sex. Little boys are encouraged to be adventurous, expected to get into trouble and to get themselves out of it. Little girls are more protected, and expected to turn to an adult for help. In school, teachers often exaggerate sex differences. Phrases such as 'two strong boys to carry the desk', 'a responsible girl to sit with the infants', 'sit quietly like the girls', 'he's a cissy', 'she's a tomboy' are common. It has been estimated that, at school, pupils are classified by sex approximately 20 times a day (Buswell, 1981). Thus children learn the stereotypes of girl and boy, and how they are supposed to behave.

Many researchers have found that teachers, both male and female, tend to spend more time talking to boys than to girls in class. In our society, males are considered more important and interesting than females (if you doubt this, consider the three-to-one ratio of male to female characters found both in children's story books and on prime-time television (Czaplinski, 1976; Durkin, 1985; Tuchman, 1978)). Spender (1982) has argued that both staff and pupils bring this assumption of male precedence with them into the classroom, and it results in boys demanding and teachers conceding them a disproportionate amount of attention.

Dweck *et al* (1978) examined not only the amount of time teachers spent with each sex but also what they said and in what context. They found that boys got both more praise and more blame than girls. However, when boys were told off it was usually for their (mis)behaviour; when they were praised it was usually for good work. Dweck argued from this that boys learned that they could perform well academically, and if they did not do well it was probably because they were misbehaving or not trying. Girls on the other hand didn't get told off much, but when they did it was usually for poor work. Their praise was mainly for good behaviour, often compared with the behaviour of the boys. So girls learned that their work was not always adequate; and since this could not be attributed to lack of effort or attention it must be due to some failing in themselves. They lost confidence in their academic ability. Dweck attributed this phenomenon to 'learned helplessness'. She went on to demonstrate that it was not an intrinsic female quality but a definite response to the teacher's behaviour. In her experiment, both girls and boys who were praised for performance and told off for behaviour gained confidence; both girls and boys who were told off for performance and praised for behaviour lost confidence.

Child-rearing practices which diminish girls' self-confidence may be particularly detrimental to their science education. Ormerod (1981) found that both girls and boys tend to rate physics and chemistry among the most difficult subjects at school. But whereas boys will prefer subjects and choose to study them in spite of their difficulty, girls tend to prefer and choose the subjects they think are easier. Even girls who achieve good results in physical science seem to lack the self-confidence to choose these difficult subjects. Harding (1981) has shown that girls do worse on multiple choice tests – which again require self-confidence to pick one correct answer – than on structured or essay-type tests, which allow more room for qualification and hesitation.

Boys may be more willing than girls to continue science even though they find it difficult because they see it as relevant to their future careers. Both girls and boys give interest in the subject and relevance to a career as the principal reason for choosing science (Kelly, 1981). But whereas boys tend to over-emphasize the importance of science for careers (choosing it 'for career reasons' when, for example, they want to be a lawyer or an accountant), girls tend to under-emphasize it (not choosing science when, for example, they want to be a nurse or a hairdresser). Informed careers advice at school could help to remedy this, but it is often a matter of too little and too late. Most schools provide some careers guidance for fifth formers, but this is seldom extended to third-year pupils making their subject choices. It is no use telling a fifth-form girl who wants to be a radiographer that she should have studied physics – by then it is too late. For girls with less traditional ambitions, careers advice can be a decided hindrance. As Benett and Carter (1981) have demonstrated, careers staff often discourage a girl who says she wants to be an engineer or an electrician, and emphasize the difficulties she will face rather than the rewards of the job.

Girls may also be discouraged from studying physical science by its masculine image. A glance at science textbooks shows numerous examples concerned with guns, cars, football and machinery – all topics which interest boys more than girls. The vast majority of illustrations in textbooks show men or boys. The *Great Scientists* series of posters is prominently displayed in many school laboratories and contains only one woman, Marie Curie; unlike the men, she is shown surrounded by her family. (The Equal Opportunities Commission has now produced a series of posters of women scientists to balance the picture.) On the

GIST (Girls into Science and Technology) project we asked children if they knew anyone who worked in a scientific or technological job; they named twice as many men as women. In mixed schools most of the physical science teachers and most of the pupils studying science in the senior school are male.

The GIST project also found that at the age of 11 a substantial number of boys but very few girls agree with statements like 'a woman could never be a great scientist' or 'girls don't need to learn about electricity or light'. If boys believe that science is a male domain this may affect their behaviour in class. It is frequently observed that boys tend to dominate the laboratory space and equipment, leaving girls only a peripheral role as note-takers or onlookers [. . . .].[1] Pupils and teachers alike accept this as normal behaviour. Moreover, where boys control the equipment, girls have less opportunity to benefit from experimental work. [. . .]

It is obviously easier to challenge the masculine image of science at a girls' school than at a mixed school. At girls' schools the physical science staff are more likely to be women, and all the senior pupils studying science are girls; the lessons can be geared to girls' interests without fear of disruption by the boys. Not surprisingly, DES statistics (1975) show that a higher proportion of girls study physical science and mathematics in girls' schools than in mixed schools of a comparable type – even though girls' schools frequently have less adequate laboratory provision than mixed schools. However, co-educational schools have other advantages, and most girls will continue to be taught in them. One strategy for reducing sex stereotyping in a mixed school is to separate the sexes for some subjects. Smith (1984) reports an experiment along these lines in mathematics. He found that the girls' attitudes and achievements both improved. Perhaps the same arrangement would be beneficial in science.

In most schools children have to choose at the end of the third year which subjects to continue for CSE or O level and which to drop. Pupils are usually about 14 years old when they make this crucial decision, and many are still going through the crisis of puberty. They are trying to establish what it means to be a woman or a man, which behaviour is appropriate and which inappropriate. It is very difficult for a child of this age to breach conventions, and the image of a subject as masculine or feminine may be an important influence on a child's decision to drop or continue it. Studying science fits in with boys' image of themselves; but for girls there is a conflict. Smithers and Collings (1981) have shown that girls who continue with science into the sixth form often consider themselves rather unattractive and unfeminine.

However, subject choices do not have to be made at this age. One school which decided to adopt a common curriculum to 16, with all pupils studying both physical and biological science, found that the proportion of girls in the A level physics class increased from 10 per cent to 40 per cent after the change. Many of these girls said that they would have dropped physics at 15 if they had been allowed to. When they had no choice but to continue it beyond the critical period of puberty, they voluntarily took the subject. The combination of masculine image of science and an inappropriate timing of option choices seems to be a powerful factor in dissuading girls from science.

Physical science not only has a masculine image but also an impersonal image. Schoolchildren think that science has to do with things, rather than people. Much of what they learn in science appears abstract and theoretical with little connection to their daily lives in the present or the future. Again this image may be more off-putting to girls than to boys. Caring for people, both physically and emotionally, is an important part of the female role, and a subject which apparently ignores people can seem irrelevant to girls' concerns. Of course science does affect our daily lives in numerous ways – but this is not usually made clear in science lessons. In recent years several 'science and society' type syllabuses have been developed which explore the social implications of science. But these have been aimed principally at sixth formers and college students, or at less able fourth and fifth formers. The science and society approach has had little impact in the early years of secondary school before children make their option choices. Yet this is the stage at which it is arguably most crucial.

These three factors – girls lack of self-confidence, the masculine image of science and the impersonal approach of science – are probably chiefly responsible for the failure of physical science to attract girls. All of them can be tackled to a certain extent within the education system, although it is important to realize that the problem of girls in science cannot be divorced from the wider issues of sex stereotyping and women's position in society. Some individual schools and teachers have had considerable success in encouraging girls into physical science by curriculum revision, careers advice, parental involvement and personal approaches to promising pupils. The Association for Science Education has a working party on girls and science, and regional groups of teachers working on curriculum material. Tameside LEA has appointed two science teachers with special responsibility for girls to advise other teachers and implement innovations in their area. Several university and college departments of engineering and physics have arranged 'taster' courses for girls considering these subjects. Probably the most wide-ranging intervention is the GIST project, which is working with teachers in eight co-educational comprehensive schools in Greater Manchester to devise and implement a range of strategies to change attitudes.[2] [. . . .] The next decade will show whether measures like these will be enough to improve the image of science in girls' eyes, and lead to greater participation by women in all aspects of scientific and technological life.

Notes

1. See Chapter 8, this volume.
2. See Chapter 11, this volume.

References

Benett, Y. and Carter, D. (1981). *Sidetracked? A Look at the Careers Advice given to Fifth Form Girls*, Equal Opportunities Commission.

Buswell, C. (1981). 'Sexism in school routines and classroom practices', *Durham and Newcastle Research Review*, Vol. IX, pp. 195–200.

Czaplinski, S.M. (1976). 'Sexism in Award Winning Picture Books'. In Children's Rights Workshop (ed.), *Sexism in Children's Books*. Writers and Readers Publishing Cooperative.

Department of Education and Science (1975). *Curricular Differences for Boys and Girls*. Education Survey 21, HMSO.

Durkin, K. (1985). *Television, Sex Roles and Children*. Open University Press.

Dweck, C.S., Davidson, W., Nelson, S. and Enna, B. (1978). 'Sex differences in learned helplessness: II The contingencies of evaluative feedback; III An experimental analysis'. *Developmental Psychology*, Vol. 14, pp. 268–76.

Gray, J.A. (1981). 'A biological basis for the sex differences in achievement in science?' In Kelly, A. (ed.), *The Missing Half: Girls and Science Education*. Manchester University Press.

Harding, J. (1981). 'Sex differences in science examinations'. In Kelly, A. (ed.), *The Missing Half: Girls and Science Education*. Manchester University Press.

Kelly, A. (1976). 'Women in physics and physics education'. In Lewis, J.L. (ed.), *New Trends in Physics Teaching: Volume III*. UNESCO.

Kelly, A. (1981). 'Choosing or channelling?' In Kelly, A. (ed.), *The Missing Half: Girls and Science Education*. Manchester University Press.

Ormerod, M.B. (1981). 'Factors differentially affecting the science subject preferences, choices and attitudes of girls and boys'. In Kelly, A. (ed.), *The Missing Half: Girls and Science Education*. Manchester University Press.

Smith, S. (1984). 'Single sex setting'. In Deem, R. (ed.), *Co-Education Reconsidered*. Open University Press.

Smithers, A. and Collings, J. (1981). 'Girls studying science in the sixth form'. In Kelly, A. (ed.), *The Missing Half: Girls and Science Education*. Manchester University Press.

Spender, D. (1982). 'The role of teachers: what choices do they have?' In Council of Europe (ed.), *Sex Stereotyping in Schools*. Swets & Zeitlinger.

Tuchman, G. (1978). 'The symbolic annihilation of women by the mass media'. In Tuchman, G., Daniels, A.K. and Benét, J. (eds), *Hearth and Home: Images of Women in the Mass Media*. Oxford University Press.

2 A model to link personality characteristics to a preference for science

John Head

Introduction

In recent years there has been a steady accumulation of evidence that personality and allied affective factors play a crucial role in determining subject choice and student success. Unfortunately, this evidence has tended to be fragmentary, a collection of separate, discrete pieces of information lacking a synthesizing theory to provide cohesion and predictive power. The few models which have been developed to date may have been correct as far as they go but are clearly incomplete. For example Roe (1952), Eiduson (1962) and McClelland (1962) suggested that male scientists often experienced a lonely childhood, perhaps suffering social isolation through illness or family circumstances, so that they developed a strong interest in their surrounding material world and a below average interest in other people and relationships. Maslow (1966) and Hudson (1966 and 1968) saw science as providing an emotionally undemanding activity appealing to boys moving from the calm of latency to the turbulence of adolescence. Even if these descriptions are valid they still leave open a number of questions, particularly why the same mechanisms do not operate with girls.

Arising from the evidence in the literature and from our empirical studies at Chelsea College it is now possible to offer a model which is compatible with all the evidence and which also has considerable predictive potential.

What we know about persons choosing science

The evidence for an association between personality characteristics and an interest in science has been more fully reviewed by Head (1979). We need now only take note of the most salient features.

Source: European Journal of Science Education (1980) Vol. 2, pp. 295–300.

The most obvious one is that of sex differences. The predominance of males, is particularly in the physical sciences and engineering, throughout the Western world can no longer be satisfactorily attributed to cognitive differences, which are too small, nor to institutional factors. Equal opportunity in education and employment has not made science any more popular with women.

Furthermore, the characteristics of those students who do opt for science show clear sex differences. Male scientists, both science students and mature, professional scientists, tend to be emotionally reticent, disliking overt emotional expression in others and themselves, and depending upon their partners in personal relationships to take the emotional initiatives. They will also tend to be authoritarian, conservative and controlled in their thinking. These differences can be seen quite early on; we have found boys aged 14 years who were opting for science to be significantly more authoritarian than their peers. Girls choosing science are not particularly emotionally reticent or rigid in their thinking, although they do seem to have low self-esteem in terms of being socially and sexually attractive.

We also know that at about the age of 13 a very high proportion of boys are attracted to science and scientific careers. Thereafter, there is a steady decline of interest in science and this disillusionment extends right through the secondary-school years and into the undergraduate period. In contrast, only a minority of girls express an interest in science at any age but there is no obvious swing from science in the middle and late teens.

Some further evidence has come from our use of sentence completion tests with secondary-school pupils as part of our research programme at Chelsea. Analysis of these responses provides further information on sex differences and between those opting for different subjects.

For example, girls at the age of 12 and 14 years seem to take a more mature attitude to personal relationships, seeing their complexity and reciprocal nature, while boys are more exploitive. In relation to the sentence stem 'A girl and her mother . . .', girls often produce responses like 'often go through a bad patch for a year but once they learn to understand each other, become the best of friends' or 'can help each other with their problems'. Similar questions, when asked of boys, tend to produce banal responses or exploitive ones, for example the parent is seen as the source of money. In contrast, boys seem to have a firmer self-identity and a clearer ambition showing more insight in response to sentence stems such as 'My main problem is . . .' and 'He/she felt proud that . . .' Such findings give us some clues about the characteristics of boys and girls of these ages.

If we compare boys of 14 years of age who opt for science with other boys, we find that the former have very cut-and-dried views on many issues. For example, they take the view that 'criminals should be severely punished' or that 'anyone who is unpopular deserves his fate'. To the sentence stem 'When a child will not join in group activities . . .', these boys gave responses like 'he is selfish', 'he must be stupid', 'he deserves to be unpopular'. In contrast, other boys and most girls pondered the possible causes and ways of integrating the child into the group. The science boys seemed to possess few doubts or uncertainties, they offered clear-cut answers.

It was this evidence which suggested the possible model for subject choice in terms of ego-identity achievement.

Ego-identity in adolescence

This model was originally postulated by Erikson (1965) and then developed by Marcia (1966 and 1976).

Erikson suggests that at different phases of life an individual faces a particular psycho-social problem which needs to be resolved before moving on to the next phase. For adolescents the acquisition of a clear ego-identity is the crucial task. At the beginning of adolescence, the individual is a dependant within the family and the school. By the end of adolescence he needs to make choices about career, life-style, personal relationships and ideologies. The ego-identity of that person is shaped by these choices. Erikson does not suggest that the development of an ego-identity is a once-and-for-all issue. Some problems about identity arise with the young child in the context of home and school, and others occur in later life, for example on retirement. Nevertheless, adolescence is the time when ego-identity development inevitably dominates the personal development of the individual for a while. The adolescent does not, however, need to achieve a clear ego-identity on all topics at one time. He may have a clear identity in respect to his career but still be unresolved in regard to personal relationships and ideology. In this article we are concerned with ego-identity achievement in respect to career.

Marcia has put more detail on the Erikson model and suggests that in going from the initial ego-diffusion condition to that of having achieved ego-identity,

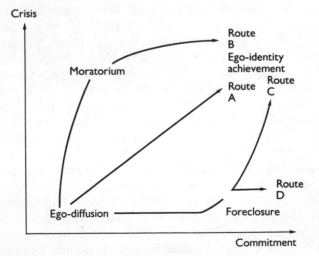

Figure 1.   Possible routes to ego-identity achievement.

two processes are involved: *crisis* and *commitment*. Crisis in this context describes a period of intensive self-examination in which one's beliefs and values are re-examined. Commitment means that the individual has acquired clear and firm beliefs both about himself and the world. Figure 1 indicates a number of possible routes to ego-identity achievement. A person may undergo crisis and commitment simultaneously and progress by route A. An alternative is to undergo a period of considerable self-doubt and self-examination in which all one's beliefs tend to be very fluid, a period known as moratorium, before acquiring beliefs for oneself and ego-identity is achieved (route B). A further possibility is that the individual may, at least for a time, hold onto beliefs and values taken without question from others, for example parents, teachers, peers. This condition is known as foreclosure. Eventually these persons might have to face up to a period of crisis, of self-examination, and so achieve ego-identity by route C. However, foreclosure does offer an escape route and an individual might postpone indefinitely any real self-examination by clinging rigidly to his beliefs and values (route D).

Ego-identity and choosing science

We can now make the link between this model of adolescent development and subject choice in schools.

For boys at the foreclosure stage, science is likely to be appealing. The physical sciences in particular offer a conventional career choice which is likely to win approval from parents, teachers and peers. They will tend to regard the overt expression of emotions, including much such expression in the arts, as being soft and feminine. Science, with its masculine image, makes little emotional demand on an individual and seems to offer clear, precise answers to problems. Opting for science will permit and possibly reinforce emotional reticence.

For a girl at the foreclosure stage the situation is very different. There is evidence that girls tend to be socialized into adult roles more through their potential of becoming a mother and housewife than through their career (Douvan and Adelson, 1966). Furthermore, these girls will tend to go into a career with a feminine image, one which already attracts many girls. Consequently, very few girls at the foreclosure stage will enter science unless they receive considerable encouragement and a model to do so from their parents and their school.

Neither boys nor girls at the moratorium stage are likely to be attracted to the science that is usually presented in our schools. They are at a stage when they are likely to be concerned with a variety of complex issues; the meaning of life, the existence of God, ideologies, their emerging sexuality, their future career and life-style. Too often science is seen as being purely instrumental with nothing to contribute to these debates. Science, somehow, seems to be scarcely relevant to the most important issues in our life.

A proportion of both boys and girls at ego-identity achievement stage will choose science. In fact, most girls entering science are probably at this stage as they will need some self-examination and sense of commitment to make this unconventional choice. However, only a minority of adolescents will have reached the ego-identity achievement stage at the age when most pupils have to make crucial decisions about subject choice at school.

This model seems to explain our observations. A large number of boys, particularly at the foreclosure stage, are initially attracted to science but there is a drift away throughout later adolescence as they undergo some crisis. The preponderance of boys at the foreclosure stage will yield the rigid, authoritarian attitudes often associated with scientists. The few girls who enter science will not usually show these foreclosure characteristics.

Effects of curriculum changes

The real use of this model linking personality development to subject choice is that it allows us to make predictions about how pupils might react to changes in school science curriculum and school organization. We can consider three posssible changes:

(1) *Delaying subject choice:* Britain is unusual in asking pupils to make crucial choices about subject options in the 13–16 age range. These decisions can only be reversed with great difficulty. What effect would delaying the choice make?

In the development through the years of adolescence the number of foreclosure pupils will diminish, hence the recruitment of boys into science would be cut. More boys and girls will have reached the ego-identity achievement stage and a proportion of these will go into science. Overall there would be a reduction in the number of students choosing science, but those who do so choose will be more likely to stay happily in the subject and to possess more flexible minds. The quantitative loss would be met by a qualitative improvement.

(2) *Giving science a more feminine image:* It is sometimes argued that science textbooks are sexist in showing illustrations of boys, rather than girls, doing practical work in the laboratory, and so forth. What effect would a deliberate attempt to change this image have? It might make it easier for girls at the foreclosure stage to accept science, so recruitment might increase. Some of these girls might, however, drift away again when they reach their crisis period. Unless the change in image was immense, boys would probably not be affected, science would still be an obvious, acceptable choice for a boy. Overall there would be some increase in the recruitment of girls, but no qualitative improvement.

(3) *Emphasizing the applications and relevance of science:* To obtain a major qualitative improvement to recruitment in science with more girls and

with students possessing imaginative, flexible minds it would be necessary to make science appealing to boys and girls at the moratorium stage.

In that event science must be seen to be relevant to the issues which concern them. The probable implication is that science would need to be presented in the context of the needs of society and individuals. Probably a case-study approach involving the application of science, and the interaction with other disciplines, would be needed. Our knowledge about the girls' concern with personal relationship suggests that the introduction of some elements of the social sciences into the case studies might prove attractive.

Is it possible to change school science in this fashion and still preserve the essential character of science itself? Clearly there would need to be some drastic pruning of content. Perhaps science teachers should not attempt to cover their subjects so comprehensively. A history teacher is content to cover the history of one country or continent over a few decades. Perhaps we must make similar choices.

It is interesting to notice that the Association for Science Education (1979) policy statement in Britain and the proposals on school physics coming from the Institute for Science Education (IPN) in Kiel are advocating such changes. The difference is that we are now offering a formal psychological model to suggest that if we want to reduce the current encapsulation of science, if we want to recruit a different sort of student, then certain curriculum changes are needed.

References

Association for Science Education (ASE) (1979). *Alternatives for Science Education*.
Douvan, E. and Adelson, J. (1966). *The Adolescent Experience*. Wiley.
Eiduson, B. (1962). *Scientists: Their Psychological World*. Basic Books.
Erikson, E.H. (1965). *Childhood and Society*. Hogarth Press.
Head, J. (1979). 'Personality and the pursuit of science', *Studies in Science Education*, Vol 6, pp. 23–34.
Hudson, L. (1966). *Contrary Imaginations*. Methuen.
Hudson, L. (1968). *Frames of Mind*. London, Methuen.
Marcia, J.E. (1966). 'Development and validation of ego identity status'. *Journal of Personality and Social Psychology*, Vol. 3, pp. 551–8.
Marcia, J.E. (1976). *Studies in Ego Identity* (unpublished monograph).
Maslow, A.H. (1966). *The Psychology of Science*. Harper and Row.
McClelland, D.C. (1962). 'On the psychodynamics of creative physical scientists'. In Gruber, H.E., Terrell, G. and Wertheimer, M. (eds), *Contemporary Approaches to Creative Thinking*. Atherton Press.
Roe, A. (1952). *The Making of a Scientist*. Dodd Mead.

3 An object relations account of the differential involvement of boys and girls in science and technology

Jan Harding and Michael Sutoris

Introduction

The focus on sex differences
Interest in the investigation of sex differences in general, dormant in much of the first half of the twentieth century, has recently been rekindled. It may not be insignificant that such interest has been associated in this century and the last with a period of vigorous and articulate movements towards sex equality (Sayers, 1982). When evidence of some newly determined sex difference is reported in the UK the newspapers generally claim this gives support for the *status quo*.[1] Such response creates concern that, in focusing on sex differences, we may be providing further ammunition for attacks on women's potential which arise from simplistic interpretations of the evidence without a corresponding questioning of underlying assumptions. In spite of this we feel it is essential to review the evidence and seek explanations.

Cognitive abilities
As far as differences in cognitive abilities are concerned, several reviewers have commented that the established differences are few, unstable and small (Fairweather, 1976; Maccoby and Jacklin, 1980; Hyde, 1981). Hyde, for example, demonstrates that the largest differences are in spatial abilities, but even in these the sex of the individual contributes only 4 per cent to the total variance in populations.

Following the publication of Hyde's paper, Rosenthal and Rubin (1982) subjected her data to further analyses. They argue that a difference reflecting only 4 per cent of variance may be associated with one group performing 60 per

Source: A shorter version of this paper appeared in Lehrke, M., Hoffman, L. & Gardner, P.L. (eds) (1985). *Interests in Science and Technology Education.* Institut für Pädagogik der Naturwissenschaften (IPN), Kiel, West Germany.

cent above the average compared to 40 per cent for the other group; this is therefore a not insignificant predictor of behaviour. However, these figures for spatial ability would match the situation in the USSR, where around 40 per cent of engineers are women, rather than in the UK, where the figure is less than 1 per cent.

Rosenthal and Rubin also investigated any change in sizes of sex differences over the last 20 years and found that these have moved in the direction favouring females 'rather faster than the gene can travel'. However one looks at the cognitive data it seems that males and females are, or are becoming, much more alike than they are different. The seeker after explanations of sex differences in science/technology involvement in the Western world will find shifting ground in models constructed from a biological base to cognitive abilities as presently conceived.

In spite of this similarity in cognitive abilities, large sex differences in the practice of science and technology persist. Whenever choice is offered in the curriculum, as happens in most Western countries at some stage of the educational process, girls and young women choose against these subjects.

Attitudes and interests: no simple correlation with science choice
The concern to measure attitudes to, and interest in, science and technology stems from an assumption that the former influences choices made for or against the latter. Certainly girls, internationally, showed less positive attitudes than did boys to science when tested in the IEA study (Kelly, 1978). Less favourable attitudes to technology were reported from girls than from boys in a survey carried out in the UK (Page and Nash, 1980). But we are not justified in assuming that differences in attitudes lead to different choices. Several studies have shown that attitudes, interests and expectations are sex differentiated even among those who *choose* science. We have Ormerod's early study (1971) which showed that among pupils choosing science the perception of it as having social implications was significantly greater for girls than for boys. An evaluation carried out in the Harvard Project Physics programme (Walberg, 1967) assessed interests by asking high school students following the course to report on how much time they spent on a number of out-of-school science-related activities. Five factors emerged from a factor analysis of these reports. No sex differences were found in factors labelled as 'Academic' and 'Cosmology', while two factors: 'Nature Study' and 'Applications to Life' loaded higher for the girls. The largest sex difference occurred, however, in 'Tinkering' which accounted for 35 per cent of the variance in the sample and on which girls showed a very low loading.

Although Smithers and Collings (1981) demonstrated that female A level physical scientists tend to show characteristics similar to Hudson's (1966) male science students (for example, they were less person-orientated than average girls), Head's (1980) work indicated a personality differentiation among those who chose science at 13+. The girls' group contained a disproportionate number of more mature girls (using Loevinger's measures of maturity) while among the boys there was a significant number of the least mature.

   An analysis of entries to National Design Competitions in the UK showed
that boys and girls might end up working on similar technical solutions to
problems, but their entry points and reasons for tackling the problem, and even
how they saw the problem itself, were rather different (Grant, 1982).

   It would seem from the above that adolescents' perception of science and
technology is not unidimensional. Boys and girls may relate to science and to
other aspects of the world in different ways so that a positive choice for science
may result from very different attitudes to it.

Further empirical work
We noted that whereas social class had differentiated groups in the National
Child Development Study up to the age of 16, when choice of career was
investigated at this age, sex differentiated more strongly than class (Fogelman,
1979). Girls aspired to caring and clerical work across social classes, while
engineering showed a similar pattern for boys.

   We were intrigued that women reaching top management position in big
American companies reported having no brothers and being close to their
fathers (Henning and Jardim, 1979); that topics in early secondary school
science which pupils labelled 'girls' science' included a tangible product, in the
absence of which girls went to great pains to decorate their notebooks (Ebbutt,
1981)

   We were puzzled that different methods of assessment appeared to favour one
sex or the other. Were the gains shown by males compared to females when
performance in multiple choice items was compared to that in extended answers
due solely to the males' lower verbal skills as claimed by some (Murphy, 1982)?

The need for a model
It was considerations such as these which led us at Chelsea College to look more
closely at object-relations theory of ego development and related work. We
found useful insights in Head's paper (1980), linking ego identity with science
choice. Gilligan's work (1982) confirmed that, in matters in which so-called
moral judgements were required, the world, and the problems under
consideration, appeared different to males and females. We looked again at the
empirical work which identified factors associated with involvement in science
and with women's achievements generally to see how a model based in object-
relations theory might account for them.

   In the rest of this paper we give a brief account of object-relations theory and
show how it generates different ways of relating to the world, which are broadly
reflected in gender. We go on to show how it makes sense of empirical findings
and to emphasize implications for education and for society.

Object-relations theory

One of the most attractive possibilities offered by object-relations theory is that
it enables us to view personality, and hence gender development, as a stochastic

process. That is to say, the particular pathway for development which occurs evolves out of the combination of the invididual plus environment (Bateson, 1973). Development may be conceived as a change from one kind of relationship between individual and environment to a new kind of relationship. Neither individual nor environment are unchanging; both become modified to some degree in the course of interaction. Thus it becomes questionable to continue to frame development in terms of cause and effect, for each component in the interaction is both cause and effect at one and the same time.

There are grounds, then, for arguing that there is no 'cause' as such of gender differences; rather, gender differences reflect different patterns of object-relating which emerge out of different combinations of infant plus child-care environment, which in turn propose certain developmental pathways rather than others. Object-relations theory offers us a model for understanding how crucial 'turning points' in human development set the pattern for different developmental pathways according to the specific contexts in which they arise.

The roots of object-relations theory

Object-relations theory is a branch of psychoanalytic theory which grew out of the work of Klein (1932), who first emphasized the importance of objects to the developing personality. It makes a number of departures from classical Freudian psychoanalysis, the most radical of which are to be found in the writings of Fairbairn (1952), which was informed by his work with adults. The work of Klein strongly influenced Winnicott (1958), for many years a paediatrician, who drew attention to the importance of the caretaking environment for the eventual development of a mature personality.

The word 'object' is a blanket term for people, aspects of people or symbols of people; inanimate objects also fall under this heading, as do less tangible aspects of the environment with which the person interacts (such as 'science'). We will briefly outline the object-relations account of development and then consider how it can inform our understanding of gender development. It should be borne in mind, however, that this summary necessarily reflects our own interpretation of theory, which derives from a synthesis of the work of Winnicott and Fairbairn.

An object-relations account of healthy development

In object-relations theory, bodily processes constitute paradigms for mental processes: in Winnicott's terms, mental life consists in the imaginative elaboration of physical experience. The link with biology is maintained, but in a way which conceives biological and mental functioning as two different levels of experience, related in a logical sense, but not directly as Freud sought to demonstrate. In view of the focus upon relationships, object-relations theory traces development not in terms of the sequential progression through a series of stages (as, for example, in instinct theory) but in terms of the changing characteristics of the individual's relationship with objects, specifically the parent-infant relationship. Unlike such stage theories, which regard the seed of development as somehow sown in the individual and waiting to grow, object-relations theory rather views the individual as a seed sown in the environment. Healthy development can only occur if the environmental conditions are favourable (in Winnicott's terms, 'good enough').

The caretaker-infant unit

At the beginning, the infant merely represents a potential for growth and development. It is dependent upon the caretaker's provision of a facilitating environment for this potential to grow into a person. Just as the infant is dependent upon the caretaker's provision of milk for physical growth, it is dependent upon the caretaker's loving care for psychological growth.

'Loving care' means protecting the infant from impingements, sensitive, adaptive management of the environment, meeting the infant's needs (emotional as well as physiological) to ameliorate the experience of frustration, distress, etc. In short, to identify empathetically with the infant.

As yet the infant is not aware of this loving care nor anything else of the world outside. The adaptive provision of the caretaker at first is so complete that Winnicott says that the infant and maternal care together form a unit. But in order for the infant to separate itself, it must discover the world outside that unit and establish for itself a place in it. The caretaker's adaptive meeting of the infant's needs includes the presentation of the right kind of object at the right moment.

Activity, feeling real, and control

The world is met and sensed through movement: 'The impulsive gesture reaches out and becomes aggressive when opposition is met . . . there is reality in this experience' (Winnicott, 1958, p. 217). The word aggression here is almost synonymous with activity, writes Winnicott; it can only be experienced when bodily functions are involved, whereas pleasure, for example, can be experienced imaginatively without the involvement of bodily functions.

With the caretaker's help the infant develops the ability to use its aggression to manipulate objects, to derive a sense of control over them, to begin to act purposefully towards them, and to begin to meet its own needs in a context where activity leads to 'control'.

The infant thus gradually becomes less dependent upon the object-presenting and protecting of the caretaker. The development of control and the strengthening of the ego enables the infant to do without the actual presence of the caretaker for longer periods of time and so to begin to separate itself out from the infant-caretaker unit. It is important that the caretaker matches this need with a gradual de-adaptation of total care.

The development of sense of guilt and a capacity for concern

Winnicott emphasizes two functions of maternal care and two corresponding roles of the caretaker. One is the caretaker as the object of the infant's urgent, excited and impulsive needs, from whom the infant takes in stuff, whom the infant empties and 'destroys'. The other is the caretaker as the supportive adaptive ego of the infant's quieter moments who receives what may be called the infant's affection. At first, the infant is unaware that these two functions belong to one and the same caretaker, but gradually, with good-enough help, there is a coming together of the two aspects of the caretaker in the mind of the infant.

Awareness grows in the infant that the ruthless consuming or taking in response to its impulsive needs may destroy the same caretaker whose supportive care it values. At this point it is essential that the environment caretaker 'survives', is there to receive an offering of affection or reparation when the infant has worked through the complex mental processes following its excited impulses. As this 'benign circle', as Winnicott calls it, is repeated day after day the infant builds up a technique to handle the ambivalence created. It first feels anxiety, but as confidence in the survival of the caretaker develops and opportunities for reparation are offered, the anxiety is held and becomes a sense of guilt.

Again, if things go well, the guilt is itself held and there develops an active concern for the environment-caretaker. The infant begins to assume responsibility for the destructive elements of its excited impulses. Confidence grows, too, in its ability to make amends. The infant not only has need of external objects, it feels concern for them. We may say that the infant develops empathy which eventually brings with it a capacity to act as an adaptive ego for someone else. As Winnicott says, the beginnings of these processes are established in the first year, but they are tenuous and if the environment fails at any time in the future, before maturity is firmly established, earlier dependent patterns re-emerge so that guilt and concern are lost.

When support is not 'good enough'
Support within the infant-caretaker relationship may fail in two main ways: the adaptive caretaker may not 'survive' to the infant in which case *separation-anxiety* develops. On the other hand, the caretaker may not de-adapt to an extent that the developing infant needs and *merging anxiety* develops.

Separation anxiety
If the adaptive caretaker fails to survive, the infant is driven to find what satisfaction and comfort it can from whatever substitutes are available (thumb, soother, etc.). The accompanying sense of frustration serves to intensify the need so that the infant comes, not merely to need the contents of the object, but to possess the object. The opportunity to use aggression in taking-in gives just this quality to the experience, and if the infant feels that it possesses the object, it can come to terms with the destructiveness of its need and the separation anxiety which it engenders. If this pattern becomes established for the infant, its object-seeking becomes predominantly a search for substitutes upon which it can depend, and so avoid the destruction of the 'good provider' which the adaptive caretaker has come to represent. But this means that the infant comes to depend more and more upon its substitutes.

The objects which the infant then possesses are therefore extremely valuable, and come to form part of the infant's self and are regarded as contents. Giving therefore is difficult for the infant in this situation because giving involves parting with contents with an attendant sense of impoverishment and separation anxiety. For such infants, taking, rather than giving, is a feature of object relations.

Merging anxiety

When the caretaker persists with adaptive functions beyond the time when the infant begins to need to take them over for itself, the infant's attempts at separating out from the caretaker-infant unit becomes complicated by a further ambivalence towards the caretaker. The frustration engenders hate and hate means destruction. To separate out means to destroy the caretaker. If the active/aggressive move to external objects is also thwarted, the infant comes to feel its aggression has destroyed these also and aggression is repressed. The infant attempts to relieve the ambivalence by becoming compliant with a corresponding loss of a sense of being real. The anxiety that develops is that of being overwhelmingly merged into the caretaker. External objects now take on a special significance, for they offer a possibility of escape from the overwhelming caretaker and they tend to become idealized.

The development of gender

We may now consider the question of gender development. Chodorow (1978) has illustrated how the asymmetric structure of parenting in which child care functions are performed almost exclusively by women produces quite different social contexts for girls and boys.

There is a tendency in our societies for boys to be pushed out of the dependent relationship before they are adequately equipped to take over adaptive functions for themselves. There is a corresponding tendency for mothers to identify more closely with their daughters, to maintain the dependent relationship for longer and to continue with their adaptive functions for themselves. Chodorow concludes that the effects of these different experiences of parenting produces a 'relational capacity' in girls which is underdeveloped in boys.

In the case of boys, the effect of being pushed out of the dependent relationship early is equivalent to the failure of the mother to survive and promotes separation anxiety. From the boy's point of view, it is his emotional dependence upon the caretaker which is destructive, and so he will tend to keep his emotions inside, and to meet his emotional needs by controlling and possessing objects which he can use as substitutes for the adaptive caretaker.

Aggressive, taking relationships will be a feature of boys' object relations. The capacity for concern may be constrained in several ways: the greater encouragement to activity that Archer and Lloyd (1982) observed in mothers and infants dressed as boys may enable the 'feeling real' and a development of a sense of control, but the opportunity to experience the quiet moments with the caretaker will be reduced and with it the opportunity to make reparation. On the other hand, if aggression and destruction is tolerated in little boys the need to make reparation is reduced and again a capacity for concern fails to develop adequately.

In the case of girls, the adaptive caretaker survives thus enabling a capacity for concern to be established and the empathy that goes with it. Giving relationships, reparation and the constructive use of aggression will be much more of a feature for girls. But the mothers held a girl child closer (Archer and Lloyd, 1982) and persisted in adaptive functions. Thus, although this means that daughters are more likely to be ready to emerge from their dependent relationship in their own time, it means also that they will be hindered in their progress beyond this point. Although they may be ready to separate, the caretaking environment maintains the state of being merged. It is not separation anxiety, but merging anxiety that would appear to be the lot of girls. A corollary of this is that autonomy in girls is much delayed.

A prediction of the analysis of gender presented here is that, contrary to the account of Eichenbaum and Orbach (1982), women emerge as the more emotionally developed of the sexes. Chodorow makes clear the nature of the links between the capacity to nurture and provide a nurturing environment for some one else and the achievement of object-relations based on giving together with the ability to participate in reciprocal relationships. This, as we have seen, implies relating to the object as an external object and involves the idea of empathy and of making a contribution rather than use of the objects for one's own ends.

The frustration which women experience in society, in their aspirations and their day-to-day living, stems from their experience of merging anxiety in a world in which they are treated as dependents. Their economic dependence upon men, or their dependence upon 'experts' who tell them what is best for them is, at an emotional level, equivalent to being merged in with these objects. Their experience is one of compliance, the sense that the world is to be fitted in with at the expense of their own personal life and public achievement. Despite this disadvantageous position in the social sphere, object-relations theory would suggest that in terms of personal life, women tend to reach further along the developmental road towards maturity than do men.

Discussion

Before turning to science we may find support for the differing views of self and the world held by two apparently well-adjusted bright 11 year olds, Jake and Amy, discussed in Gilligan's study (1982). Jake described himself by giving his name, where he lived, what his father did and went on to say:

> I like corny jokes. I don't really like to get down to work, but I can do all the stuff in school. Every single problem that I have seen in school I have been able to do, . . . but sometimes I don't want to waste my time on easy homework. Most people I know I like, and I have a good life, pretty much as good as any I have seen, and I am tall for my age.

While Amy responds:

> Well, I'd say that I was someone who likes school and studying, and that's what I want to do with my life. I want to be some kind of scientist or something, and I want to do things, and I want to help people . . . I think that everybody should try to help somebody else in some way, and the way I'm choosing is through science.
>
> (p. 34)

As Gilligan points out, Jake defines himself by separating himself out from the world, while Amy locates herself in relation to the world. But it is Amy and not Jake who wishes to be a scientist. We will return later to Amy's choice of science. Meanwhile, it is interesting to note Fairbairn's observation (1952, p. 6) that scientific pursuits are associated with individuals who feel detached from the world, but value in science the opportunities it presents for 'controlling' ('orderly arrangement and meticulous accuracy'). The possession of scientific 'knowledge' or 'fact' would be an admirable substitute for a boy suffering separation anxiety to depend upon: it cannot be denied (i.e. destroyed); it establishes order in an incomprehensible universe and so contributes to his sense of security by enriching his sense of self if he possesses the knowledge.

Where science is presented in schools as factual, with abstracted laws and concepts to be learned (and this is how HMI (1980) observed physics and chemistry in a sample of schools from year 3 upward), then it is not surprising that it appeals to boys. But perhaps it appeals particularly to boys who, as a result of 'not good-enough' nurturing, are emotionally immature (Head, 1980) or whose preferred mode of operating is convergently (Hudson, 1966). This fits also with the picture emerging from Roe's study (1953) of famous male scientists, many of whom experienced some traumatic period of separation, sometimes through illness, in early childhood. Head's current work suggests that those who score high on autonomy measures but low on intimacy form the largest proportion of boys.

Some girls may choose science for the security it seems to offer and perhaps Smithers' and Collings' (1981) girls who saw themselves as less attractive and were less person-oriented are among them. But for most girls their confrontation with hard 'scientific' facts offers little scope for change or reparation and suggests one has to 'fit in' – learn the laws. If science is something that has to be taken-in and accepted and not denied, then it presents a sense of merging-in, which is a source of anxiety in many girls. The report of Ward (1975) that girls found technology something huge that frightened them supports this view.

Girls with a capacity to relate empathetically to *external* objects do not have the same need as boys to abstract from and possess their sure and certain aspects. In this we may see an explanation for the identifying of science activities with a tangible product as 'girls' science' and the importance of decorating their books – external objects (which Ebbutt (1981) explains in terms of aesthetic appeal).

Their greater connectedness to the world through external objects means that every event is enmeshed in a complex web of inter-relationships; girls and women may continually be processing information from a much greater range of sources than do boys and men. This may be at the root of women's so-called intuition. It also means that science presented as an interpretive, rather than a controlling activity, is more likely to appeal to girls.

Physical science and technology are not usually presented in an interpretive mode. Indeed, the recent emphasis in Britain in micro electronics and its presentation in courses such as 'Control Technology', is a clear example of an approach fitting the male perspective rather than that of the female. Such courses offer few opportunities to 'make a contribution' (Winnicott, 1965), to give or to be creative. Some girls have been enabled to see science and technology in these terms, hence the greater association of the recognition of social implications of science, and its applications to life, to its choice by girls (Ormerod, 1971). Amy sees it as a way to fulfil her desire to help others. Many girls in Britain studying A level sciences have chosen them with a medical career in mind and a similar purpose (Smithers and Collings, 1981). The girls entering for design competitions see technology as serving their caring concerns; for the boys, the solving of the technical problem itself may be more rewarding, contributing as it does to a sense of control (Grant, 1982).

If a different view of science underlies girls' choice of it, how is this reflected in women's practice of science? 'Anna Brito' is reported to have said that the difference lies not in the kind of science developed but in the choice of problem to work on (Goodfield, 1981), but she is critical of the aggressive, controlling approach to cancer treatment and appeals for a more gentle, 'collaborative' handling of patient and disease. There are also intriguing indications of an empathetical identification with the blood corpuscles she was studying. She *knew* the lymphocytes were hiding somewhere. The same message comes over even more clearly in Evelyn Fox Keller's (1983) account of Barbara McClintock and her work: 'A Feeling for the Organism'. Perhaps a different kind of science *is* possible . . . ?[2]

From this one may argue that humanity needs more women in science and technology. To effect this it would be a mistake to focus on ways of 'changing' girls in order to induct them into science. Rather we must consider the pupil in relationship with science and technology and ask how we might go about providing a facilitating environment in order to develop this relationship in the direction of reciprocity and creativity.

Before concluding our discussion of the explanatory and predictive power of object-relations theory, let us focus on two aspects of female achievement. First, in connection with assessment techniques for public examinations, women's greater connectedness to the world through external objects may account for their greater facility with 'open', extended answers to examination questions

(Harding, 1981). These will enable them to explore the complexity of a problem more comfortably than through multiple choice items. This latter form of assessment does not allow one to express reservations, to indicate the influence of context or to say: 'Well, it depends . . .' The characteristic of multi-choice questions is that they focus on a single right answer, abstracting the only possible solution from limited data – an activity matching more closely a male mode of operating, as described in this paper, than a female one.

Secondly, Hennig's and Jardim's account (1979) of successful business women showed them to be more distant from their mothers and closer to their fathers. Fathers form important external objects for girls when the mother is the primary caretaker. The women concerned tell stories of their childhood that show nurturing was good enough to enable them to separate out, to develop independence and a sense of self-worth (which many of the women seeking abortion advice in Gilligan's study had not).

We may succeed in attracting more women into science, but women will not succeed in science (or any other sphere) in greater numbers unless we provide girls with opportunities to develop autonomy. The desire to protect daughters carries with it a stunting of their development and potential. In so far as the desire to protect daughters conceals the mother's dependence on the relationship for her own sense of identity, we need to provide women with alternative ways of valuing themselves. Satisfying work outside the home is one way of providing this, which brings us again to concern that women may enter more readily into science and technology education to obtain the qualifications that much available work requires.

Notes

1. Examples are:
   Observer, 27.9.81, 'Must Boys Be Boys?', Nigel Hawkes, Science Correspondent.
   Sunday Times, 10.1.82, 'Is It Your Brain that Makes You Male or Female?', Bryan Silcock.
   The Standard, 7.12.83, 'Happy to be Prisoners of Gender', Reporter: Jeremy Campbell.
2. Keller claims that the popular association of maleness (in terms of impersonal and objective functioning) with science is a limiting concept of scientific activity as it has been carried out by men and women. Like Head, she sees the presentation of science in this way acting as a filter in attracting into science more males with these characteristics. She turns to object-relations theory to account for the differentiation of males and females into 'objective' and 'personal' ways of relating to the world. (See Keller, E.F., 'Women, Science and Popular Mythology'. In Rothschild, J. (ed.) *Machina Ex Dea*. Pergamon Press, 1983.)

References

Archer, J. and Lloyd, B. (1982). *Sex and Gender*. Penguin.

Bateson, G. (1973). *Steps to an Ecology of Mind*. Granada (Paladin).

Chodorow, N. (1978). *The Reproduction of Mothering – Psychoanalysis and the Sociology of Gender*. University of California Press.

Ebbutt, D. (1981). 'Girls' science, boys' science revisited'. In Kelly, A. (ed.), *The Missing Half: Girls and Science Education*. Manchester University Press.

Eichenbaum, L. and Orbach, S. (1982). *Outside In Inside Out*. Pelican

Fairbairn, W.R.D (1952). *Psychoanalytic Studies of the Personality*. Tavistock.

Fairweather, H. (1976). 'Sex differences in cognition'. *Cognition*, Vol. 4, pp 231–80.

Fogelman, K. (1979). 'Educational and career aspirations of sixteen-year olds', *British Journal of Guidance and Counselling*, Vol. 7, pp. 42–556.

Gilligan, C. (1982). *In a Different Voice: Psychological Theory and the Development of Women*. Harvard University Press.

Grant, M. (1982). 'Prized projects', *Studies in Design Education, Craft and Technology*, Vol. 15, pp. 9–10.

Goodfield, J. (1981). *An Imagined World: The Story of Scientific Discovery*. Hutchinson.

Harding, J. (1981). 'Report on Science Examinations and the Type of School'. Paper presented to first Girls and Science and Technology Conference, Netherlands.

Head, J. (1980). 'A Model to Link Personality Characteristics to a Preference for Science', *European Journal of Science Education*, Vol. 2, pp. 295–300. See Chapter 2, this volume

Hennig, M. and Jardim, A. (1979). *The Managerial Woman*, Pan Books.

HMI (1980). *Girls and Science*. Matters for Discussion, No. 13, HMSO.

Hudson, L. (1966). *Contrary Imaginations*. Methuen.

Hyde, J. (1981). 'How large are cognitive gender differences?', *American Psychologist*, Vol. 36, pp. 892–901

Keller, E.F. (1983). *A Feeling for the Organism: The Life and Work of Barbara McClintock*. W.H. Freeman and Co.

Kelly, A. (1978). *Girls and Science*. IEA Monograph Studies No. 9, Almqvist and Wiksell International.

Klein, M. (1932). *The Psycho-Analysis of Children*. Hogarth.

Maccoby, E. and Jacklin, C. (1980). 'Psychological sex differences'. In Rutter, M. (ed.) *Scientific Foundations of Developmental Psychiatry*. Heinemann.

Murphy, R. (1982). 'Sex Differences in Objective Test Performance', *British Journal of Educational Psychology*, Vol. 52, pp. 213–9.

Ormerod, M.B. (1971). 'The social implications factor in attitudes to science', *British Journal of Educational Psychology*, Vol. 41, pp. 335–8.

Page, R. and Nash, M. (1980). 'Teenage attitudes to technology and industry', Report: Standing Conference on Schools' Science and Technology, 1 Birdcage Walk, London SW1H 9JJ.

Roe, A. (1953). *The Making of a Scientist*. Dodd Mead.

Rosenthal, R. and Rubin, D. (1982). 'Further meta-analytic procedures for assessing cognitive gender differences', *Journal of Educational Psychology*, Vol. 74, pp. 708–12.

Sayers, J. (1982). *Biological Politics*. Tavistock Publications.

Smithers, A. and Collings, J. (1981). 'Girls studying science in the sixth form'. In A. Kelly (ed.), *The Missing Half: Girls and Science Education*. Manchester University Press.

Walberg, J. (1967). 'Dimensions of scientific interests in boys and girls studying physics', *Science Education*, Vol. 51, pp. 111–16.

Ward, J.P. (1975) 'Adolescent girls and modes of knowledge', *Educational Review*, Vol. 27, pp. 221–8.

Winnicott, D.W. (1958). *Collected Papers: Through Paediatrics to Psycho-Analysis*. Tavistock.

Winnicott, D.W. (1965). *Maturational Processes and the Facilitating Environment*. Hogarth.

4　Some issues in the historical construction of the scientific truth about girls

Valerie Walkerdine

Preamble

The issues which I will raise in this paper address certain questions both about history and how to approach 'scientific fact' in relation to data on young girls' performance in mathematics.

My excursions into history are the result of my attempts to examine the historically specific nature of psychological evidence about sex differences. What concerns me is both the generation of theory, subsequent empirical findings and the complex interplay of ideas about science and maths and ideas about girls and boys.

It is quite common for those who take liberal positions within psychology and feminism to argue about sex or gender bias in the generation and interpretation of data. Such people may regard biology as a reactionary category, either to be shunned in favour of 'environmental' explanations or taken as an uncomfortable but incontravertible fact. However, such approaches do not ask the strategic question about what counts as scientific truth and how to approach the issue of truth and, therefore, of fact. It can clearly be demonstrated that truth is not a timeless and unchanging matter. However, my interest here is to show how certain explanations for girls' performance have currency now. And, more particularly, therefore, as both an issue for psychology and for feminism – how can we evaluate the 'truth'. The examination of its historical constitution and the moments at which certain statements which pre-exist the emergence of psychology become incorporated into scientific theory are very important aspects of such work.

Some current evidence about girls

In her evidence to the Committee of Enquiry into the Teaching of Mathematics (The Cockcroft Committee), Hilary Shuard cites historical evidence about the

Source: Paper presented at Second International Conference on Girls and Science and Technology, Norway, September 1983. First published in this volume. © Open University, 1987.

mathematical education of girls. She quotes from the 1929 Report on the Teaching of Mathematics the evidence of a headmistress:

> A teacher of girls is, perhaps, too easily satisfied when her pupils are working steadily and conscientiously along the lines which she has laid down for them: a boy is almost cetain to go off at a tangent . . . routine does him less harm, because he is less susceptible to its influence. Probably one of the weaknesses of girls is that they will submit to so much dullness without resentment . . . Many girls who are, apparently, good workers are mentally lazy, they reproduce, but they do not produce.

We could, of course, pass such a statement off as mere history, assert that things have changed. However, not only is it common to hear such statements made by current teachers, in almost identical terms, but Hilary Shuard herself says 'the evidence cited later in this appendix shows that some of the reasons given for the girls' need of mathematics in the 1912 report are now advanced as reasons for their failure to perform better at the subject' (p. 275). Shuard reviews some of the evidence which demonstrates not only that girls are well behaved and hard working in the classroom, but that they also perform better on those aspects of mathematics which are taken to require low-level rule following. The implication is that we can take such factors as these to account for the phenomenon of 'girls' failure in mathematics'.

The issue which concerns me is first, how is it that attributes which, on one level, might be considered good qualities, industriousness and diligence, are understood as a cause of girls' failure in mathematics; and second, how are such accounts presented as scientific evidence.

How to read the data

The issues which will form the central focus of this examination are the way in which certain observations made about girls both in relation to their classroom performance and to results on mathematical tests are presented as 'hard evidence'. For example, when confronted with the evidence that girls are, indeed, well behaved, diligent, and so forth, it is hard to discount such data especially when it accords so nicely with, so to speak, the 'evidence of our own eyes'. Similarly, when Hilary Shuard states that

> The items on which girls did significantly better were easier, with an average success rate of 64 per cent, as against an average success rate of 49 per cent for the items on which boys did significantly better

> (Cockroft Report, p. 277)

it is difficult to treat these statements as anything other than scientific fact. The figures refer to an analysis carried out by Shuard of the sex differences in performance on a mathematics survey given to over 2,000 ten year olds in England and Wales (Ward, 1978). Shuard goes on to say that girls performed better than boys in 11 out of 91 items while boys performed significantly better than girls in 14 items. This means that, in fact, on 66 out of 91 items there were no statistically significant sex differences, and girls did significantly better than boys in 11 items as well. However, since those items on which girls did better were 'easy' then we are led to think that girls are 'only' good at those aspects of mathematics which are low level and indeed Shuard (1981) states this. Girls' 'low level skills' are taken to be produced by rule following, rote learning and not 'proper conceptualization, real understanding'. From this we understand their performance as not really good at all.

The same slippage occurs in a review by Geoffrey Howson of Walden and Walkerdine's *Girls and Mathematics: The Early Years* (1982). Howson's statements about our 'misinterpretation' of 'hard facts' have led me to ask how we should approach the question. 'Is it true that girls only follow the rules (whereas boys have access to proper conceptualization)?' In order to answer this question I shall attempt to demonstrate that:

1 'Rule following' and 'proper conceptualization' are oppositions which are relatively recent and emerge in relation to post-war changes in mathematics education, particularly with regard to the interrelation of developmental psychology and mathematics in which mathematics becomes reasoning: a developmental process to be understood as relating to the mind of the child. In other words mathematics and reasoning are *naturalized*.

2 The naturalization of reason, which is scientized within the domain of psychology, places the site of reason in *the body*, but the male body; the female body being excluded.

3 Thus the opposition needs to be understood in relation to the history of developmental psychology and I would assert that it is axiomatic that it would be *girls* who are understood as following the rules.

4 The production of the female body (and later the female mind) as the object of a psychology permits the production of a psychological object. I use the word produce because I want to suggest that the theory does not simply *represent* something real and underlying and material but that the way a science selects its objects and draws its boundaries actually constructs its own truth conditions, limits and parameters. It is this naturalized body and mind which are taken to be the simple cause of attainment. That is, when we produce evidence in which sex differences in attainments are posited, they are both produced within, and interpreted according to, assumptions about ability as directly causal.

Cognitive development

The body of theory which is used to explain performance in mathematics in the primary school is based on ideas derived from theories of cognitive development. This means that successful maths performance is taken to be produced by the attainment of concepts of particular *stages* of logical thought, etc. According to this view of learning, *real understanding* (based on concepts) is contrasted with *rule following* or *rote memorization* which is in the scheme of old theories and practices of maths teaching, and is success produced without the solid foundation of real understanding. (An easy example is the contrast between being able to chant one's tables and understanding multiplication as cumulative addition.)

It is, therefore, axiomatic to the view of maths learning that is dominant in primary schools that proper success is produced on the basis of real understanding. So success is judged in terms of the mastery of concepts in a mode of practice designed to promote and produce 'real understanding' – learning through activity, not chanting tables, etc. Success at maths is taken to be an indication of success in reasoning. Maths is seen as *development* of the reasoned and logical mind. This is where the important issue of girls' success arises. Those explanations which *allow* girls' success at all say that it is based on rule following, rote learning and not proper understanding.

Hence, they negate that success: girls 'just' follow rules; they are good compared with 'naughty' boys who can 'break set', that is, make conceptual leaps. Girls are good at computation and we know this to be low level, etc. Everything which heralds the success also testifies to it as failure: something which amounts to nothing.

This explanation is totally *internal* to the theory about the production of reason and rationality: girls may be able to do maths, but it's not 'proper' maths they can't properly 'reason', and therefore this is taken to account for later failure where 'abstract reasoning' is required. The explanation of girls' failure cannot be understood as external to the explanation of reason in general, which is taken to be something which boys possess (even though they are not necessarily doing as well at maths).

Interestingly then, in the case of girls, as in all judgements about attainment, attainment itself is no longer seen as a reliable indicator. Following from this, right attainment can, in principle, be produced for wrong reasons. It becomes important, therefore, to establish as permissable only that attainment taken as premised on 'real understanding'. Only this attainment then is *real*. The rest, though apparently real, is false. Counting girls' performance as evidence is not distinct from the issue of what it is taken to be evidence of. We have not only to debate about the data but also to engage with why this distinction is made at all and what it means, as well as its *effects* in terms of *practical consequences* for girls' education.

I am not arguing that there is is no problem for girls, but rather that in order to approach the practical implications, we have to identify the precise nature of the problem. I am trying to demonstrate that the problem is not really as simple as reading the truth from an analysis of hard evidence. I want to ask not *are the arguments true* – but how is this truth constituted, how is it possible, and what effects does it have? Using arguments derived from Foucault (1977), I think we can begin to deconstruct this truth about girls – to see it for what it is, a production.

Reason and gender

My argument, in a nutshell, is that ideas about reason and reasoning cannot be understood historically outside considerations about gender. Since the Enlightenment (indeed well before that), reason, or the cogito, has been deeply bound up with attempts to control nature. The rationality of the cogito was taken to be a kind of re-birth, the birth of the rational self, in this case without the intervention of a woman. The rational self was in this sense a profoundly masculine one, from which the woman was excluded, her powers not only inferior, but subservient. The 'thinking' subject was male; the female provided both the biological prop to procreation and to the servicing of the possibility of male control.

The doctrine was extremely widespread and I mention it here only to raise certain issues. A fuller discussion may be found in Easlea (1980). Perhaps the best-known example of such a philosophy is in the work of Rousseau, who described a 'reasoning woman' as a monster. However, what I am particularly concerned with here is the transformation of a philosophical doctrine into the object of science in which reason became a capacity invested within the body, and later mind, of the man and from which the female was excluded by definition.

The development of science from the seventeenth century was intimately connected to the control of nature by man. From the nineteenth century, particularly with the work of Darwin, the human was also accorded the status of natural (rather than God given). 'Human Nature', therefore became the object of scientific enquiry. That scientific enquiry was from its inception deeply patriarchal. It legitimated doctrines which existed previously as philosophy. With the transformation of this doctrine into a science the female body and mind both became objects of the scientific gaze. In this way it began to be possible to make 'true' statements about female nature – no longer an object of debate, but one resolvable by resort to evidence. Yet 'female nature' does not pre-exist the development of those doctrines, bodies of knowledge and scientific practices which produced it as its object. The truth of scientific statements is in this sense not discovered: it is produced.

We can monitor the *effects* of such 'facts' on the fate of particular girls and women. For example, the legitimization of their exclusion and of practices of discrimination could now be based on fact: the proven inferiority of girls and women. It was quite common in the nineteenth century to exclude women from higher education and the professions on the grounds that they were swayed by their emotions and not, therefore, invested with the capacity to make rational judgements.

It is from arguments such as this that the sexed body (the seat of 'nature') becomes the site for the production and explanation of mind. Since the very differentiation between men's and women's bodies is central to this approach, there is no way that reason can ever be gender neutral.

It shows how we arrive at the common sense notion we have today that 'women's minds' are incompatible with hard sciences and maths. Often social psychologists are content simply to state that these are the views that women and men, girls and boys have about feminity, masculinity, etc. Helen Weinreich-Haste (1981) reproduces for us the 'common sense' which accrues from such discourses. She asked students and school children to rate science and scientists – hard/soft, masculine/feminine, etc. These bi-polar constructs, of course, are already given in the 'common sense' of which I have spoken. It is not surprising, therefore, that science was seen as 'hard, intellect based, complex and masculine'. However, what is also important is that there was no 'feminine discipline' cluster – arts were not seen as feminine either. In similar ways, as with science, woman is externalized from the arts – as Griselda Pollock and Rozika Parker have shown so well in their study of women and art in *Old Mistresses* (1981).

What is important, I think, is that although such work as Weinreich-Haste's gives us valuable information, we need to understand how such views came to be held. Otherwise we are left with the quasi-scientific idea that such views are 'incorrect' and, therefore, attitude change is needed to modify them. I think this plays down the way in which these sets of attitudes about women are related to central conceptions about science and rationality itself.

Woman as the object of nineteenth-century science was gentle, not profound, the holder of the moral order, mothering. The picture it painted was of the weak and fainting women of the Victorian middle classes, whose butterfly minds were unable to concentrate – moving from a little embroidery to a little this, a little that, gentle accomplishment but no profundity. It certainly matters that individual women may not have fitted this 'stereotype' but what is equally important is that no woman was able to stand outside the power of that scientific truth. Women could resist that power – they could dare to be different. But the necessity to struggle and the form that struggle took was completely bound up with undermining that truth. And the placing of the account in women's bodies immediately placed them naturally external to a capacity to reason. So I am stressing the importance of not seeing this as a distortion or a simple mistake but as a productive force which had effects.

Developing from this poor, frail, moral woman whose failure to reason was produced through incapacity and not oppression, we come to the arguments which see it as physiologically dangerous for women to reason. They were endangering the future of the species by engaging in the strain produced by such an unnatural act, unnatural because women's bodies were so unsuited to such activity. By the twentieth century, we see such a view encapsulated as, for example, in Felter's article in Education Review 1906: he argued that for girls to use up energy at puberty in intellectual work would endanger the development of their reproductive organs, producing the possibility of infertility and thus endangering the 'species'.

What a burden, therefore, girls and women had to bear. Now they were not only harming themselves; they were also endangering the future of the species. With such moral imperatives, opposition would be made difficult for girls and it is not surprising that those who opposed would become hard, masculine-like women of dubious sexuality and the target of scorn and perjorative evaluations.

It is important in this respect that, since women became the guardians of the future species, they were kept in private at home. In the nineteenth century, bourgeois women were systematically excluded from participation in the public domain: their one job became mothering. Working class women continued to work outside the home, but this was considered a danger, a threat associated with the problems arising out of the 'deviance' of the dangerous classes. Keeping women in the home became a moral and scientific imperative at every level.

But, of course, *men* had no physiological bars to reasoning – they were not endangering the future of the species — indeed we imagine that for them there was a moral imperative to reason. They, unlike the women, had the responsibility to control the public domain.

The proliferation of difference – and the siting of that difference in the muscles, nerves, body of the woman – grounded her inferiority and the necessity that she be protected, by men. It also kept women out of competitive spheres – e.g., intellectual life and politics. Again, therefore, I stress the *positivity* of the discourse. If these arguments helped to produce practices of *exclusion* of women, they had material effects. Practices of discrimination and exclusion were produced and backed up by science.

In addition, it is also possible to demonstrate why particular struggles on the part of women took the form which they did. If women were excluded from various public spheres, by being confined to the domestic, then clearly resistance by certain groups of women would be about gaining entry into the barred fields of educaton, the academy, and politics.

Women's resistance, therefore, took the form of being allowed to enter examinations – to prove themselves equal to men. Cambridge local examinations were opened to girls in 1863. Women had to prove themselves equal to men – rational like men. They had to fight on the same terms, and could not change them.

Conclusions

It is not my intention to suggest that girls have no problems in being successful in mathematics and science. Rather, I have tried to engage with and challenge the grounds on which that success is produced and understood. We still do have to explain why some girls in the classroom are judged to follow the rules and work hard. We still have to address differences and discontinuities in performance. But if we shift the grounds on which we address these issues we might begin to look elsewhere for answers. By examining the conditions which have set the parameters of masculinity and femininity, which have naturalized these states in support of the division of labour, we can begin to challenge not only that truth but the practices which make its continuity possible.

References

Cockcroft, W.H. (1982). *Committee of Enquiry into the Teaching of Mathematics in Schools: Mathematics Counts*. HMSO.

Easlea, B. (1980). *Witchcraft, Magic and the New Philosophy*. Harvester.

Felter, W.L. (1906). 'The education of women', *Education Review*, Vol. 3, pp. 351–63.

Foucault, M. (1977). *Discipline and Punish: The Birth of the Prison*. Allen Lane.

Howson, G. (1982). Review of Walden and Walkerdine, *Education*, Vol. 159, No. 11, p. 188.

Parker, R. and Pollock, G. (1981). *Old Mistresses*. Routledge and Kegan Paul.

Shuard, H. (1981). 'Mathematics and the Ten Year Old Girl', *Times Educational Supplement* (27/3), p. 40.

Walden, R. and Walkerdine, V. (1982). *Girls and Mathematics: The Early Years*. Bedford Way Papers, No. 8, Heinemann.

Ward, M. (1978). *Mathematics and the Ten Year Old Child*. Evans/Methuen.

Weinreich-Haste, H. (1981). 'The image of science'. In Kelly, A. (ed.), *The Missing Half: Girls and Science Education*. Manchester University Press.

Part II

Teachers and Classrooms

5 The biasing influence of pupil sex in a science marking exercise

Margaret Goddard Spear

Introduction

[. . .] Most attempts to account for sex differences in science uptake and science achievement employ some combination of psychological, social or educational explanations. The study reported here focuses upon educational factors and in particular, the role that teachers might play in discouraging girls from the physical sciences. Teachers who consciously or unconsciously believe that the physical sciences are masculine subjects are likely to perceive girls as unsuited for science studies. This view could colour the teachers' expectations regarding girls' prospects in the science subjects. A large body of literature exists demonstrating the importance of teachers' expectations upon their pupils' self-perceptions, behaviour and general school attainment (Davidson and Lang, 1960; Rist, 1970). Reports relating specifically to science are very scarce, but the findings of a small pilot study by Rowell (1971) suggest that teachers' expectations can either reinforce or counteract girls' under-achievement in science.

The expectations of teachers might also be reflected in the subjective evaluation of pupils' classroom performance and work submitted for assessment. Work of a high standard which has been produced by a girl might be assessed harshly because it is inconsistent with a teacher's preconception that science is a subject for boys, whereas comparable work produced by a boy might be overrated as it conforms to the teacher's expectations.

Circumstantial evidence and anecdotal reports (Kelly, 1981) suggest that some science teachers hold greater expectations for the boys in their classes than for the girls, and that these different expectations do, on occasions, lead to differential treatment of boys and girls. But, speculation and opinions apart, evidence relating to the possible biasing influence of pupil sex upon science teachers' expectations and evaluations is lacking.

Source: *Research in Science and Technological Education*, Vol. 2, pp. 55–60, 1984.

To provide some objective data regarding teacher response to pupil sex, an investigation was undertaken to determine whether or not secondary science teachers display sex bias in their subjective evaluations of the written work of pupils. Two hypotheses were tested:

1. for identical written work, science teachers award higher marks to boys than to girls;
2. based on the evidence of written work, science teachers form higher expectations for boys than for girls, as signified by their judgement of pupils' potential for science.

Sample

The science departments of 22 comprehensive schools in the south of England were contacted and 11 agreed to assist in the study. Replies were subsequently received from most of the science teachers in the majority of the participating departments. The sample consisted of 55 men and 25 women. A comparison of their age and principal teaching subject distributions with national distributions [. . .] indicated that the sample was respresentative of secondary school science teachers with respect to these statistics.

Procedure

The experimental procedure required the teachers to evaluate six samples of work on the topic 'Distillation'. The samples were xeroxed copies of authentic handwritten accounts and were all easily legible. They were presented as having been written by 11-year-old pupils following a combined science course. Each sample described a different arragement for producing distilled water. Two of the samples were conceptually accurate, two of them contained correct ideas but some of the experimental details were faulty, and two were scientifically incorrect. Thus the samples covered a range of different experimental methods, different levels of attainment, and different styles of presenting work. Three of the samples had originally been produced by girls and three by boys. However, each sample was presented to half of the teachers as being the work of a girl and to the remaining teachers as being the work of a boy. This arrangement was plausible since the samples could not be readily associated with either sex, according to the results of a previous study (Spear, 1982). Pupil sex was denoted by the inclusion of the word 'male' or 'female' at the top of each work sample. To explain the presence of such an unusual term on a child's piece of work, the samples were described as having been specially prepared. The pupil's age was also included to add further credence to this claim.

Booklets were formed by stapling together the samples, an introduction and instructions. The order of the samples, which was fixed, attempted to reproduce the sort of mixture of standards that a teacher might encounter in a typical pile of exercise books. However, in half the booklets the first sample was written by a 'male', whereas in the other half the same first sample was attributed to a 'female'. Each booklet contained three samples written by 'boys' and three by 'girls', arranged alternately.

The introduction presented the marking exercise as follows:

> The object of the investigation is to compare the standards set by teachers, and also the importance that different teachers place on a variety of work characteristics.

To validate these ostensible objectives, when the teachers were asked evaluative questions at the end of each work sample, they were offered no framework criteria.

The instructions requested that the teachers should not discuss or consult with each other. To check that they had not surmised the real objectives of the study, the teachers were encouraged to write comments on the aims and/or design of the investigation. Many comments, often lengthy, were received from respondents, but there was no indication that any respondent had guessed the real aim of the investigation.

At the end of each work sample appeared ten questions. Three of the questions referred to 'this boy's work' or 'this girl's work'. Together with the 'male' or 'female' tag appearing on each work sample, these were the only signs alerting the teacher to the sex of the pupil

The first question requested the subject to grade the work sample on a scale of A−F. This alphabetical scale was later converted to a numerical scale, where A=1, B=2, etc. The next seven questions inquired into a number of work variables which, according to a previous study (Spear, 1982), teachers believe may differ between boys and girls. The last two questions referred to the pupil's interests in science and suitability for O level physical science courses as implied by the quality of the work sample. Subjects indicated their responses to these last nine questions on a five-point scale, where one was the highest rating possible and five was the lowest.

Results

Preliminary analysis revealed that male and female teachers both tended to differentiate between the work of a boy and the work of a girl in similar ways. Thus all the results reported refer to the mixed sex sample of 80 science teachers.

Mean grades awarded to 'boys' and 'girls' for each item on each individual work sample are recorded in Table 1. It can be seen that work attributed to a boy received a higher mean rating for 'richness of ideas' in all six samples. Additionally, in all six samples, a 'boy' author was judged to display greater interest and greater O level suitability than a 'girl' author. Work attributed to a boy also received higher mean ratings for 'scientific accuracy', 'organization of ideas' and 'conciseness' in five of the samples. The only work characteristic on which girls were favoured was 'neatness'. They received higher mean ratings for five of the six judgements of 'neatness'.

Table 1 shows a clear tendency on the part of the teachers to overrate the work of a boy compared with that of a girl. Forty-six of the 60 comparisons recorded in the table display this trend, with work attributed to a boy receiving a higher mean rating than the same work when attributed to a girl. If pupil sex was an inconsequential variable, one would expect boy's work to receive higher ratings in half of the comparisons. To determine whether the observed frequency differs significantly from this expected frequency, χ^2 was calculated. The value obtained was 17.07, which is significant at the 0.1 per cent level.

Having hypothesized that higher marks would be awarded to the work of a boy than to the work of a girl, a one-tailed t-test was used to determine the significance of the difference between the boy's means and the girl's means. Fifteen of the 60 comparisons were significantly different at the 5 per cent level.

Table 1. Mean grades awarded to 'boy' and 'girl' on each variable for each sample of work.

Variable	Pupil sex	Sample					
		1	2	3	4	5	6
Overall grade	Boy	4.22	2.37*	3.63	2.11*	4.47	1.95
	Girl	4.38	2.86	3.60	2.43	4.29	1.97
Neatness	Boy	2.76	2.40	2.66	2.14	2.68	2.10
	Girl	2.90	2.34	2.56	2.05	2.64	1.97
Time and effort involved	Boy	2.39	2.45	2.74	1.62	3.16	1.43
	Girl	2.64	2.32	2.67	1.76	3.26	1.45
Scientific accuracy	Boy	4.36*	2.40*	3.55	1.98*	4.63	2.17
	Girl	4.60	2.86	3.86	2.42	4.55	2.50
Richness of ideas	Boy	3.58*	2.69	3.32	1.76	3.71	1.63
	Girl	3.90	2.87	3.60	1.97	3.90	1.71
Organisation of ideas	Boy	3.26*	2.40*	2.97	2.25	3.63	1.86
	Girl	3.60	2.82	3.10	2.30	3.62	2.03
Expressive language	Boy	3.18	2.95*	3.08	2.93	3.89	1.51
	Girl	3.35	3.32	3.29	2.87	3.86	1.61
Conciseness	Boy	3.11	2.14*	2.39	2.83	3.11	3.15
	Girl	3.33	2.47	2.55	3.11	2.88	3.18
Interest	Boy	2.39*	1.92	2.34*	1.42*	3.11	1.77
	Girl	2.94	2.13	2.98	1.68	3.30	2.08
O level suitability	Boy	3.39*	2.39	2.82*	2.17	3.45	2.20
	Girl	3.68	2.53	3.11	2.29	3.45	2.32

*Significant at the 5 per cent level.
Note. Highest possible grade was 1 and lowest was 5, hence the lower the figure the higher the grade.

This can be compared to the ratio of 3/60 which would be expected to occur by chance. The two variables which were most consistently rated significantly different for boys and girls were 'scientific accuracy' and 'interest'.

Discussion

It could be argued that the teachers' higher rating of boys' work is merely a reflection of reality. Certainly there is evidence (Kelly, 1981) that boys are more interested in science, better at science and more likely to continue studying science. However, the findings of the present study, that work attributed to a boy is rated higher than identical work attributed to a girl, must be taken into account when discussing the reasons for boys' customary superior attainment in science. The results presented above suggest that even if there are differences between boys' and girls' aptitude for science, their interest in science, their attitudes towards science, etc., teachers may be further magnifying these differences.

Besides tending to award higher marks to the work of a boy than to the work of a girl, the teachers also tended to express higher expectations for boys than for girls. The variable 'O level suitability' had been included as a direct indicator of teacher expectation. The teachers also judged the work of a boy to indicate greater interest than that of a girl. Since a pupil's interest is likely to result in greater motivation and greater strivings in both present and future assignments, interest represents an indirect indicator of a pupil's potential for science. Hence, the teachers' sex biased ratings of interest provide additional support for the view that they held higher expectations for boys than for girls.

In the past too little attention has been paid to the attitudes and actions of the science teacher. Most studies concerned with girls' position in science have focused upon differences between boys and girls. But two groups of people – teachers and pupils – are involved in science education in schools. There is no logical reason why we should attempt to explain the differential uptake and achievement of boys and girls in science predominantly in terms of differences between boys and girls. [. . .]

Acknowledgements

The work reported above was carried out as a part-requirement of an M.Ed. degree course in Science Education at Exeter University. I would like to thank my supervisors, P.F.W. Preece and C.G. Carre, for their interest and guidance.

References

Davidson, H.H. and Lang, G. (1960). 'Children's perceptions of their teachers' feelings towards them related to self-perception, school achievement, and behavior', *Journal of Experimental Education*, Vol. 29, pp. 107–18.

Kelly, A. (ed.) (1981). *The Missing Half: Girls and Science Education*. Manchester University Press.

Rist, R.C. (1970). 'Student social class and teacher expectations: The self-fulfilling prophechy in ghetto education', *Harvard Educational Review*, Vol. 40, pp. 411–51.

Rowell, J.A. (1971). 'Sex differences in achievement in science and the expectations of teachers', *Australian Journal of Education*, Vol. 15, pp. 16–29.

Spear, M. (1982). *Sex Bias in a Science Marking Exercise*. M.Ed. dissertation, University of Exeter.

6 Teachers' views about the importance of science to boys and girls

Margaret Goddard Spear

Introduction

Considerable importance is attached to science education in Britain as evidenced by recent government publications. The Department of Education and Science (1981 and 1982) advocates that science should have a place in the education of all pupils of compulsory school age. Special mention is often made of the need for equality of treatment and opportunity between girls and boys.

> A science course is an essential component of the curriculum of every boy and girl up to the end of compulsory schooling.
>
> (HMI, 1977, p. 27)
>
> Both before and after 16, care must be taken to see that girls do not by their choices limit the range of educational and career opportunities open to them. Positive steps may be necessary to encourage girls to broaden and modernize their aspirations and to feel confident of success in unfamiliar fields of science and technology.
>
> (DES, 1977, p. 12)

Much of the responsibility of encouraging girls to study science falls upon teachers, and in particular science teachers.

> It is important that school should do everything possible to show to girls as well as boys the importance and relevance of the physical sciences and to encourage girls to study them.
>
> (HMI, 1979, p. 199)

Besides offering curricular and careers guidance to pupils, teachers are also expected to supply information and advice to the pupils' parents (DES, 1977).

There are several implicit assumptions common to the government publications referred to above. For instance, (a) teachers believe that the study of science subjects makes a valuable contribution to girls' education, (b) teachers,

Source: Paper presented to Third International Girls and Science and Technology Conference, England, 1985. First published in this volume. © Open University, 1987.

particularly science teachers, are well informed about the educational qualifications required for a wide range of occupations, and (c) teachers hold supportive views regarding girls' entrance into science-related occupations, training courses and further education courses. To date, few studies have sought to establish the validity of these assumptions. This paper describes teachers' replies to questions that refer to the importance of science education for girls. The questions were presented to the teachers in three separate questionnaires that enquired into various aspects of teachers' beliefs about different school subjects and different categories of pupils.

Samples

Three groups of secondary school teachers provided the data reported in this paper. The teachers all taught in mixed comprehensive schools located throughout the southern half of England. The schools were initially contacted by sending a letter to either the head teacher or head of science. Questionnaires were subsequently sent to those schools that expressed interest in the investigation and willingness to volunteer staff as subjects. Details of those teachers who returned questionnaires in each investigation are outlined below.

Investigation 1.   67 teachers (30 men and 37 women) from three schools. They taught a wide range of subjects.
Investigation 2.   36 teachers (16 men and 20 women) from a single school. Again, the teachers taught a variety of subjects.
Investigation 3.   62 science teachers (42 men and 20 women) from nine schools.

Results

In the first investigation, teachers of all subjects were asked about their beliefs concerning the importance of science subjects to the general education of pupils. The question was asked twice. The first time with reference to the general education of boys, and the second time with reference to the general education of girls. The two questions appeared beneath each other. The teachers indicated their responses on 4-point scales, ranging from 'very important' (scored 4) to 'not at all important' (scored 1).

The replies showed that the teachers believed that science education was of greater importance to boys than to girls. The mean ratings given to boys and to girls are shown in Table 1A. The table also contains a value for t which shows that the result is statistically significant at the 0.1 per cent level, and a value for the effect size index 'd', which provides a measure of the magnitude of the difference. ('d' was calculated by subtracting the girls' mean rating from the boys' mean rating and dividing by the standard deviation of the whole sample.)

The question asked in the first investigation referred to a rather abstract concept, the general education of pupils. It gave teachers the opportunity to

Table 1. Secondary teachers' views of the importance of science subjects for pupils.

	Mean rating				
	Boys	Girls	d	t	p
A Investigation 1 Importance to general education Judged by teachers of all subjects (N = 67)	3.82	3.58	0.50	4.51	0.001
B Investigation 2 Importance of qualifications Judged by teachers of all subjects (N = 35)	3.71	3.54	0.32	2.64	0.05
C Investigation 3 Importance of qualifications Judged by science teachers (N = 62)	3.65	3.23	0.70	6.64	0.001

Table 2. Male and female science teachers' mean ratings of the importance of science qualifications to pupils' future lives.

	Importance to:				
	Boys	Girls	d	t	p
Male teachers (N = 42)	3.54	3.05	0.79	6.17	0.001
Female teachers (N = 20)	3.85	3.55	0.68	2.85	0.01

Table 3. Percentage frequency breakdown of science teachers' responses regarding the importance of science qualifications to pupils' future lives.

	Very important	Fairly important	Not very important	Not at all important
Boys	67.8	29.0	3.2	0
Girls	33.9	54.8	11.3	0

express a theoretical view about the comparative importance of science education to boys and to girls. In contrast, the second investigation contained a question that referred to a more tangible issue. Teachers were asked how important they thought CSE/O level qualifications in science subjects would be to pupils in their future lives. Again the question appeared twice, the first time referring to girls and the second time to boys. The same 4-point rating scale was used.

Replies were received from another group of teachers of all subjects. Although the responses were less sex differentiated than in the first investigation, they still showed that the teachers considered science education to be of greater value to boys than to girls (Table 1B).

In the third investigation, a group of science teachers were given the second question referring to the specific issue of the value of science qualifications. Their replies indicated that they too believed that science education was more important to boys than to girls (Table 1C). This view was shared by both male and female science teachers (Table 2). A detailed breakdown of the science teachers' replies is given in Table 3. Although 68 per cent of the teachers considered science qualifications to be very important for boys, only 34 per cent gave a similar response for girls.

A comparison of the mean ratings and d values in Table 1 reveals that teachers' responses varied according to the teachers' subject speciality. Surprisingly, science teachers' replies to the second question were more sex differentiated than were the replies received from teachers of various subjects. This difference arose not because the science teachers over-emphasized the importance of science qualifications for boys, but because they regarded the acquisition of qualifications in the science subjects to be significantly less important for girls than did teachers of other subjects ($z = 2.42$, $p < 0.05$).

In the Department of Education and Science publication *Girls and Science* (1980) it was asserted that 'The study of physical sciences by girls should be seen primarily as an aspect of their general education and not solely as a means of encouraging them to seek careers in science-based industry' (p. 30). Yet a comparison of Table 1A and 1B shows that teachers of various subjects gave more sex-differentiated responses when considering the importance of science to pupils' general education than when considering the importance of science qualifications to pupils' future lives. It would appear that teachers need to be made more aware of the contribution that science can make to the general education of all pupils, including girls.

Discussion

The replies received from the science teachers give cause for concern. If science teachers believe that science subjects are more important for boys than for girls, then they are likely to positively encourage boys to continue their science subjects, but not be too perturbed when girls decide to drop science.

The advice and encouragement received from teachers is one of the factors that can influence a pupil's decision to study a particular subject (Benett and Carter, 1981; Nash *et al*, 1984). Thus science teachers should strive to offer pupils guidance about subject options, their career implications, and career opportunities. Regrettably, the direct involvement of science departments in curricular and career guidance is limited (DES, 1980). Thus many pupils are receiving little or no information through a potentially effective communication channel. Moreover, there is little likelihood of teachers providing more support and encouragement to girls unless they themselves have shed lingering doubts about the value of science education to girls' present and future lives. Clearly, steps need to be taken to make science teachers more aware of the importance of qualifications in science to girls.

The finding that science teachers judge the science subjects to be less important for girls than do teachers of other subjects is particularly disturbing. Not only do science teachers underestimate the importance of science for girls compared with other teachers, but they probably also underestimate the importance of science for girls compared with the girls' parents. Kelly *et al*. (1982) asked parents how important they thought it was for their child to continue various subjects when they became optional. Of the traditional school subjects, they indicated that English and maths were the most important subjects for girls, followed by physics. Physics was judged to be even more important for girls than for boys. These findings suggest that parents may hold more enlightened views regarding the importance of non-traditional subject choices to girls' educational experience and career prospects than do teachers.

Conclusion

The findings discussed above indicate that there is a need to work with science teachers to raise their awareness of the value to girls of studying science. This could be achieved in a number of ways.

1. Initial teacher training courses could
   (a) consider the value to pupils (girls as well as boys) of learning science, especially physical science,
   (b) Introduce project work on the range of occupations that require or prefer qualifications in science subject(s).
2. Individual teachers could be
   (a) informed by more systematic coverage of the topic in science and science education journals,
   (b) encouraged to attend careers seminars, conferences, courses.
3. Science departments should be encouraged to
   (a) emphasize in subject option booklets the value and appropriateness of science studies for girls,
   (b) organize careers exhibitions in conjunction with careers teachers,

(c) display posters that convey the fact that women as well as men are engaged in scientific activities,

(d) show films, videos, tape-slide sequences that illustrate careers requiring science qualifications. Surely few teachers would decline access to such resources, particularly just before the end of term?

References

Benett, Y. and Carter, D. (1981). *Sidetracked? A look at the careers advice given to fifth-form girls*. Equal Opportunities Committee.

DES (1977). *Education in Schools*. HMSO.

DES (1980). *Girls and Science*. HMI Series: Matters for Discussion No. 13, HMSO.

DES (1981). *The School Curriculum*. HMSO.

DES (1982). *Science Education in Schools*. HMSO.

HMI (1977). *Curriculum 11–16*. HMSO.

HMI (1979). *Aspects of Secondary Education in England*. HMSO.

Kelly, A., *et al.* (1982). 'Gender roles at home and school', *British Journal of Sociology of Education*, Vol. 3, pp. 281–95.

Nash, M., Allsop, T. and Woolnough, B. (1984). 'Factors affecting pupil uptake of technology at 14+', *Research in Science and Technological Education*, Vol. 2, pp. 5–19.

7 Teachers' interactions with girls and boys in science lessons

Margaret Crossman

Introduction

In the 1970s approximately 85 per cent of girls left school with very little knowledge of the physical sciences (Kelly, 1979). No doubt it was this kind of consideration which led Hodgson (1979) to comment paradoxically that the problem with girls in science was that girls were not in science. Thompson (1980) considered that the most important single factor contributing to the high sex bias in physics was the choice exercised by pupils.

I taught physics for many years in a mixed comprehensive school. The masculine nature of science (Kelly, 1985) was clearly noticeable, and I was naturally concerned about the lack of girls taking my subject to examination level. While many of the girls I taught did well in their examinations, Harding (1979) had shown that the physical sciences were becoming increasingly unpopular with girls. Dale (1974) and Ormerod (1975) found that girls in single sex schools were significantly more likely to choose physics or the physical sciences than their co-educated sisters. Ormerod *et al.* (1979) considered that it would benefit pupils studying physics up to 16+ if all girls could be educated in single sex schools, and all boys in mixed schools!

While acknowledging that the reasons for girls choosing not to study physics are many and varied, it struck me forcibly that most physics lessons were directed at the boys, and that relatively little communication went on between girls and their teachers. This could be one of the reasons why girls in mixed schools were less likely to choose physics than girls in single sex schools. If it were shown that girls were indeed disadvantaged by an imbalance in communication in favour of boys, then remedial action might be possible. Kelly *et al.* (1985) found that only 37 per cent of a sample of teachers agreed with the statement 'teachers often allow boys to dominate in mixed classrooms'. Most of

Source: Paper presented at Girl-Friendly Schooling conference, Manchester Polytechnic, September 1984. First published in this volume. © Open University 1987.

the teachers were in favour of equality of opportunity for boys and girls, but they believed that it already existed, and that there was no need to modify their own behaviour. My study was intended to explore the reality of classroom interactions between teachers and their male and female pupils in science.

The instrument and the sample

The school in which this study was conducted is a purpose-built comprehensive in one of the northern boroughs of Greater Manchester. The school is co-educational and caters for approximately 1,500 pupils between the ages of 13 and 18 years. At the time of the study it had been open for eight years, had a thriving sixth form, and enjoyed a very good local reputation. Its intake is drawn from mixed socio-economic backgrounds, and in that sense it is truly comprehensive.

The third year pupils taking part in the study were in their first year in the school. Each pupil was timetabled for one 70-minute lesson in each of the three sciences per week. Five classes took part in the study. Three were observed for both their physics and biology lessons, the fourth for physics only and the fifth for biology only. This double observation was an attempt to minimize the number of variables; unfortunately a timetable clash prevented this for the last two groups. Two of the physics classes had the same female teacher; the other two physics classes had different male teachers (see Table 1). The two classes taught by the female physicist were also taught by the male biologist. The other two biology classes had different female teachers. Thus each subject was taught equally by male and female teachers. The staff involved were all recommended by their head of department as competent teachers with a minimum of six years' teaching experience. All were teaching their own specialist subject.

Four double lessons were observed for each class in each subject. The study involved 135 pupils, 65 girls and 70 boys. The actual numbers fluctuated slightly due to pupil absences. A note was made of the boy/girl ratio in each lesson and the results were adjusted to allow for this.

A modified version of the Flanders Interaction Analysis Categories (Flanders, 1970) observation scheme was used. In this scheme classroom interaction is coded every three seconds into one of 10 categories (Table 2). This was modified

Table 1. Classes taught by each teacher.

	Physics			
	Mrs U	Mr S	Mr T	not observed
Mr X	3B3,3W1	—	—	—
Biology Mrs Y	—	3W4	—	—
Mrs Z	—	—	—	3W2
not observed	—	—	3R1	—

Table 2.   The Flanders interaction analysis categories.

Category Code	Behaviour
1	Pupils engage in constructive work either practically or mentally, with a minimum of overall confusion and concomitant teacher silence
2	Praise or encouragement by the teacher
3	Teacher accepts or develops pupil's ideas
4	Teacher asks (a) cognitive memory (recall) question (b) more complex question
5	Teacher gives facts or information
6	Teacher gives directions for procedures
7	Teacher criticizes or justifies her/his authority
8	Pupil responses (a) recall or description (b) generalizations, inferences, etc. (c) asks for clarification of teacher directions
9	Pupil initiation. Expresses own ideas, initiates new topic, develops opinions or lines of thought
10	Confusion, little or no work being done

for my purposes by using a colour coding (general–pencil; girl–red; boy–green) to indicate who was involved in the interaction. The observation interval was extended to four seconds because of the physical difficulties involved in juggling three different writing implements whilst concentrating on observing categories. It proved impossible to use a stop-watch to time intervals except when there was little variation in activity. However, after a little practice, timing became automatic and approximately 1,000 notations were obtained per 70-minute lesson. Practical work and theory were originally recorded separately, but since relatively little practical work was performed the two were not analysed separately.

Results

The results of this investigation are set out in Tables 3 and 4. Table 3 shows the overall distribution of class time in different activities, and Table 4 shows the sex differences in these activities.

Overall the greatest percentage of class time (26.5 per cent) is taken up by teachers giving out facts or information, i.e. lecturing the class. Teachers giving directions for procedures also takes up a considerable amount of time (19 per cent). This gives the impression of teacher-dominated classrooms, which is somewhat balanced by the next two largest categories: silent work (i.e. silent on the part of the teacher) (17 per cent), and pupils' responses (12 per cent).

Table 3. The perentage of classroom time taken up in different behaviours.

	All teachers	Sex of teacher Female		Male	Subject taught Physics		Biology
(2–8) Teacher talk	68.9	63.8	***	72.1	61.1	***	74.9
(8&9) Pupil talk	14.7	14.9		14.5	17.2	***	11.8
(1) Silent work	17.0	20.9	*	13.1	21.5	**	12.5
(2) Praise	1.7	1.6		1.8	1.5		1.9
(3) Acceptance	8.4	8.1		8.7	7.8		8.9
(4) Questions	8.6	9.0		8.3	9.1		8.1
(4a) memory	6.1	7.1		5.1	7.5	*	4.7
(4b) complex	2.5	1.8		3.1	1.7	*	3.2
(5) Information	26.5	22.7		30.2	16.4	***	36.7
(6) Directions	19.0	18.8		19.1	23.1	**	14.8
(7) Criticism	3.8	3.6		4.0	3.0		4.5
(8) Pupil response	12.3	12.6		11.9	15.0	**	9.6
(8a) recall	6.5	7.5		5.5	7.8	*	5.2
(8b) generalization	2.1	2.0		2.3	1.9		2.4
(8c) seek clarification	3.7	3.1		4.3	5.3	**	2.1
(9) Pupil initiation	2.4	2.2		2.6	2.3		2.2
(10) Confusion	0.4	0.6		0.2	0.2		0.6

* difference significant beyond 5 per cent level
** difference significant beyond 1 per cent level
*** difference significant beyond 0.1 per cent level

Nevertheless it is noticeable that on average the teacher talks nearly five times as much as all the pupils put together.

The most striking difference between male and female teachers is that males talk much more than females. Female teachers were one and a half times more likely to allow their classes to work constructively, either practically or mentally, for a time, without talking to the class. Apart from this, male and female teachers were remarkably similar in their distribution of class time.

Physics teachers talked less in class than biology teachers, and allowed more time for silent work. Physics teachers also allowed considerably more pupil talk than biology teachers. Looking at the sub-categories it is clear that much of the difference in teacher talk is accounted for by the far higher percentage of total time spent by the biology teachers in giving information (5). On the other hand physics teachers spent more time than biology teachers giving directions for procedures (6) – mainly in preparation for silent work. Much of the difference in pupil response is accounted for in the category of pupil seeking clarification of teacher directions (8c). Since the most obvious response to this sort of query is for the teacher to issue further, perhaps more explicit, directions, categories (6) and (8c) are to a certain extent interdependent. Although there was little overall difference in the percentage of time that physics and biology teachers spent

Table 4. The percentage of all classroom talk involving girls and boys[1]

	All teachers		Female teachers		Male teachers		Physics teachers		Biology teachers	
	girls	boys	girls	boys	girls	boys	girls	boys	girls	boys
(2-9) All interactions	22.3 ***	32.4	19.9 ***	33.2	24.7 *	31.6	24.7 ***	37.4	19.9 **	27.5
(2-7) Teacher talk	15.1 ***	22.1	13.3 ***	21.8	16.7 *	22.4	15.9 ***	25.0	14.3 **	19.2
(8&9) Pupil talk	7.2 ***	10.3	6.6 ***	11 4	7.7	9.2	8.8 **	12 4	5.5	8.3
(2) Praise	0.9	0.9	0.7	0.9	1.1	0.9	0.6 *	1.0	1.2	0.8
(3) Acceptance	3.7 ***	6.3	3.5 ***	6.8	4.0	5.8	3.6 ***	6.3	3.9 **	6.3
(4) Questions	2.8	3.3	2.6	3.6	3.0	3.0	2.5 *	4.1	3.0	2.6
(4a) memory	2.1	2.7	2.2	3.0	2.0	2.5	2.2 *	3.4	2.0	2.1
(4b) complex	0.7	0.6	0.4	0.6	0.9	0.6	0.3 *	0.7	1.0	0.5
(5) Information	1.5	1.4	0.9	1.0	2.0	1.9	1.0	1.4	2.0	1.5
(6) Directions	5.3 ***	7.0	4.8 *	6.5	5.8	7.4	7.3	9.4	3.2	4.5
(7) Criticism	0.9 ***	3.0	0.8 ***	2.9	1.1 **	3.2	0.8 ***	2.7	1.0 ***	3.4
(8) Pupil response	6.0 **	8.6	5.7 **	9.5	6.2	7.7	7.4 **	10.9	4.5 **	6.3
(8a) recall	2.9 **	4.6	3.3 **	5.6	2.6	3.5	3.4 **	5.9	2.4 **	3.3
(8b) generalization	0.9	1.6	0.9	1.6	1.0	1.6	0.8	1.5	1.1	1.6
(8c) seek clarification	2.0	2.5	1.5 *	2.3	2.6	2.6	3.2	3.5	0.9	1.5
(9) Pupil initiation	1.2	1.8	0.8	2.0	1.5	1.6	1.3	1.5	1.0 *	2.1

[1] Note that figures in this table are percentages of total classroom *talk* (categories 2–9), not percentages of total classroom *time*, as in Table 3. Figures do not sum to 100 per cent because general talk to the whole class is not shown.
* sex difference significant beyond the 5 per cent level;
** sex difference significant beyond the 1 per cent level;
*** sex difference significant beyond the 0.1 per cent level

asking questions, there were differences in the sorts of questions asked. Physics teachers were more likely to ask memory, or recall, questions, while biology teachers asked a higher proportion of more complex questions requiring more thought. Discussion with the biology teachers after the results had been processed revealed that they were trying to operate an approach whereby they presented the pupils with information and then asked them to consider it. They were pleased that objective research showed that they were succeeding in this aim.

The proportion of all classroom talk involving individual girls and boys, rather than the class as a whole, is shown in Table 4. Overall there was approximately one and a half times as much communication between boys and teachers as there was between girls and teachers. The imbalance for physics teachers was slightly greater than that for biology teachers. More noticeable, however, is the fact that the imabalance in favour of communication with boys was much greater for the female teachers than for the male teachers. Female teachers had less communication with girls and more with boys than did male teachers. Imbalances in favour of boys were present in both teacher talk and pupil talk. In both cases the differences were less marked for the biology teachers than for the physics teachers, and less marked for the male teachers than for the female teachers.

More detailed analysis of the various interaction categories shows that the largest sex difference was in category (7), criticism. Boys received over three times as much criticism from teachers as did girls. Boys were the recipients of slightly more teacher questions (4) than girls, although this difference was not statistically significant. However, there was a significant difference in category 8, where boys answered more questions than girls did. When girls were asked a question they were, in general, able to answer it. However, they tended not to answer questions unless they were specifically asked to do so. There were also statistically significant sex differences in category 3, teacher accepting or developing pupil's ideas. This may be linked to boys' greater tendency to respond; as boys answer more questions it is not surprising that their ideas are more likely to be taken up by teachers.

Most of these sex differences appeared among all four groups of teachers (male and female; physics and biology). However, it is noticeable that male teachers, while continuing to criticize boys approximately three times as much as girls, were otherwise fairly egalitarian in their treatment of girls and boys. While there was still a tendency for them to be more involved with boys than with girls, this was generally smaller than for female teachers. In both physics and biology boys were criticized more than girls, responded more than girls and had more of their ideas accepted by the teacher than did girls. In addition physics teachers praised boys more than girls and asked them more questions, whereas these trends were reversed (although to a non-significant extent) in biology.

When the results were examined in even more detail, teacher by teacher, (not shown in Tables) it was found that the smallest overall sex difference in teacher talk occurred with the male biology teacher, who was the best of a group of good teachers. A tendency was noted for pupils of the 'wrong' gender for a subject to talk more to teachers of the 'right' gender for that subject, i.e. girls talked more to male physics teachers than to the female physics teacher, while boys talked more to the female biology teachers than to the male biology teacher.

Discussion

The main results of this study are to confirm that science teachers in general interact more with boys than with girls. Teachers direct more criticism at boys than at girls, but even when criticism is left out of account teachers talk more to boys than to girls. In addition boys talk more in class than do girls. The imbalances are slightly more marked in physics than in biology, and are more characteristic of female than of male teachers.

The favouritism shown to boys in physics could mean either that communication with boys is greater than that with girls because boys generally do better in physics, or that boys do better in physics because communication with them exceeds that with girls. Whatever the cause of the imbalance, it may also have consequences. The fact that physics teachers talk more to boys than to girls in third year may be part of the reason why many girls choose not to continue to study physics in the fourth and fifth years. However, it cannot be the only factor, as more girls than boys chose to continue with biology, despite the fact that biology teachers also direct more of their talk at boys than at girls. Moreover, Stanworth (1981) has shown that even girls whom one might consider to be in a favourable position in the education system (i.e. A level students in Arts subjects) are marginalized in the classroom. Spender (1982) has examined the role of language in this marginalization, and argued that teachers face a difficult task in countering boys' demands for attention and society's assumption that boys are more noteworthy than girls. However, the fact that in this study physics teachers showed a greater tendency than biology teachers to favour boys may indicate that differences in the size of the sex imbalance are an influence on choice of subject. It would be interesting to explore this point across a range of different subjects.

One of the most surprising results of this study is the finding that female teachers were more biased towards boys in their classroom interactions than were male teachers. At the end of the last school visit, informal interviews were held with the staff involved in this study. In the interview the staff were told of the purpose of the research. One female teacher claimed that she made no distinction between boys and girls, while the other two female teachers said that they made a special effort to include and encourage the girls. These decisions are not reflected in the results obtained. If the female teachers made genuine efforts either to treat boys and girls equally, or especially to encourage girls (and there is no reason to doubt their word), then their attempts either failed or were crowned with only partial success. It is possible that the sex difference would have been even larger without such special efforts. Nevertheless it is difficult to see why the imbalance should be greater for female teachers than for male teachers (who did not seem particularly interested in the problem).

Conclusion

Most teachers seem unaware that there is an imbalance of communication in favour of boys in science lessons. Studies like this can help to increase awareness and encourage teachers to devise strategies to minimize the imbalance. it is possible that the form of communication with girls is different from that with boys, placing different demands upon and giving different signals to the two sexes. Girls and boys seem to respond differently in science (reasons may be innate or cultural) and it would be useful to explore these differences further by considering the patterns in girls' schools and in boys' schools, and comparing them with each other and with the pattern in a mixed school.

References

Dale, R.R. (1974). *Mixed or Single Sex School?* Routledge & Kegan Paul.

Flanders, N.A. (1970). *Analysing Teaching Behaviour.* Addison Wesley.

Harding, J. (1979). 'Sex differences in examination performance at 16+', *Physics Education*, Vol. 14, pp. 280–4.

Hodgson, B. (1979). 'Girls in science', *Physics Education*, Vol. 14, p. 270.

Kelly, A. (1979). 'Where have all the women gone?' *Physics Bulletin*, Vol. 30, pp. 108–11.

Kelly, A. (1985). 'The construction of masculine science', *British Journal of Sociology of Education*, Vol. 6, pp. 133–54. See Chapter 8, this volume.

Kelly, A. *et al.* (1985). 'Traditionalists and trendies: teachers' attitudes to educational issues', *British Educational Research Journal*, Vol. 11, pp. 91–104.

Ormerod, M.B. (1975). 'Subject preference and choice in co-educational and single sex secondary schools', *British Journal of Educational Psychology*, Vol. 45, pp 257–67.

Ormerod, M.B., Bottomley, J., Keys, W. and Wood, C. (1979). 'Girls and Physics Education', *Physics Education*, Vol. 14, pp. 271–7.

Spender, D. (1982). 'The role of teachers: what choices do they have?' In Council of Europe (ed.), *Sex Stereotyping in Schools.* Swets & Zeitlinger.

Stanworth, M. (1981). *Gender and Schooling.* Women's Research and Resources Centre. Centre.

Thompson, N. (1980). 'Sex differentials in physics education', *Physics Education*, Vol. 14, pp. 285–8.

8 The construction of masculine science

Alison Kelly

Introduction

[. . .] There are at least four distinct senses in which it can be argued that science is masculine. The most obvious is in terms of numbers – who studies science at school, who teaches it, who is recognized as a scientist. Secondly, there is the packaging of science, the way it is presented, the examples and applications that are stressed. Thirdly, there are the classroom behaviours and interactions whereby elements of masculinity and feminity developed in out-of-school contexts are transformed in such a way as to establish science as a male preserve. And finally there is the suggestion that the type of thinking commonly labelled scientific embodies an intrinsically masculine world view. These four arguments will be examined in turn in this paper, with particular emphasis on the least well-developed approach, that concerning classroom behaviours. [. . .]

The numbers game

Perhaps the simplest way in which science – or to be more precise, physical science – acquires its aura of masculinity, is through the numerical dominance of boys in science classes. Seventy to 80 per cent of all examination entries in physics are from males, who also form about 60 per cent of all candidates in chemistry, but only 30–40 per cent of candidates in biology. This implies that physics and chemistry classes in the senior part of the secondary school are predominantly male, a fact which is evident to junior children, and presumably influences their perception of the subjects. Also evident to pupils is the fact that men comprise about 80 per cent of physics and chemistry teachers, but only about 50 per cent of biology teachers (DES, 1983). Irrespective of the content of the lessons, these simple statistics immediately convey to children the message that this area of the curriculum is mainly for boys. [. . .]

In the Girls into Science and Technology (GIST) study we asked 11-year-old children, 'Do you know anyone who works in a scientific or technical sort of job? If yes, please tell us who it is and what they do (e.g. my sister is a motor mechanic)'. Despite the loose definition of a scientist and the deliberately

Source: British Journal of Sociology of Education, Vol. 6, pp. 133–54, 1985.

countersexist example, only 4 per cent of the pupils said they knew a women scientist compared to 26 per cent who knew a man. Boys and girls were similar in this respect. The point here is not to question whether this is a true reflection of the representation of males and females in technical work (census figures suggest that it is), but to suggest that these pupils' perceptions of their surroundings helps to foster the association of masculinity with science.

The predominance of males in science text books has been well documented, not only in this country (Kelly, 1976; Samuel, 1981; Smail, 1984; Taylor, 1979; Walford, 1980, 1981) but in places as diverse as the United States (Gaetana, 1966; Heikkenen, 1978), the Soviet Union (Kelly, 1982; Walford, 1983), Norway (Hilmo, 1983) and Holland (Lensink, 1983). Typically there are between two and 10 times as many illustrations of and references to men and boys as there are for women and girls. [. . .]

In terms of numbers, then, physical science at school is clearly male. [. . .] This numerical dominance goes some way to establishing science as masculine. Maleness is an important component of masculinity; but it is by no means the whole story.

Packaging science

Many of the authors who have analysed science textbooks have commented not only on the numbers of males and females involved but also on the way they are represented. Taylor (1979) concludes that 'references to females were few, references to active females even fewer and references to females in scientific activities were virtually non-existent'. Walford (1980) notes that textbook representations of women and girls include 'women pushing prams, a woman floating on the Dead Sea, girls blowing bubbles, women cooking, women as radiographers, nurses or patients, women used as sex symbols, women looking amazed or frightened, or simply women doing "silly" things'. [. . .]

This opens up a wider area of interest. A textbook which had equal numbers of illustrations of girls and boys but showed boys doing all the experiments with girls watching, taking notes or looking puzzled, would do nothing to undermine the masculinity of science. But what of a book that showed girls doing all the things that boys usually do? Or one that included no people of either sex? Although superficially egalitarian I would argue that both of these ideas are based on a concept of male-as-norm, which is just as powerful as (if rather more insidious than) blatant discrimination in re-inforcing the notion that science is masculine.

By the time they reach secondary school, girls and boys differ in many ways. They have different interests and hobbies, different background experiences and they envisage different futures for themselves. Girls' interests centre around people, boys' around control (Gilligan, 1982). Based on their toys and childhood hobbies boys have much greater experience than girls of tinkering activities. They are also more interested in traditional topics in physical science and more likely to aspire to a science-based job (Kelly, *et al.*, 1984). Science curricula and science books which take for granted the sorts of experiences and interests which are characteristic of boys but unusual in girls thereby help to create a science with masculine connotations. [. . .]

This sort of curriculum is not hard to find. Both Taylor (1979) and Heikkenen (1978) comment on the small number of representations of people of either sex in science textbooks. This reinforces the notion that science is about things, not people, and increases the alienation from science of girls whose socialization is primarily towards people. Topics which are presented in an abstract and theoretical way have the same tendency – boys can often see the career relevance of studying science and persevere where girls will not. Examples which concentrate on guns, cars, fooball and the industrial uses of science are similarly biased towards boys. [. . .]

This argument has been explored in detail by Smail (1984). Her aim is to develop a science curriculum for schools which takes girls' experience and world views seriously by altering [. . .] the context or packaging of science. At present science is masculine because it is presented in a certain way; if it were presented in a different way it could have a different image. The suggestion is that by utilizing girls' existing interests science may come to form part of an acceptable feminine identity. But the underlying content of science to be taught is seen as gender-neutral and remains essentially unaltered.

Re-contextualization of gender

[. . .] Adolescent girls and boys also differ in other ways which have less immediate relevance to science. These differences in behaviour and self-perceptions influence classroom interactions in science (and elsewhere). In this section I will examine the ways in which such behaviour contributes to the masculinity of science by forming an indirect link between pupils' gender identity and the school subject. This is an area which has not been widely discussed, and I will, therefore, explore this line of reasoning in rather more depth than the previous ones.

Drawing on the work of Bernstein and Bourdieu, MacDonald (1980) argues that gender is re-contextualized within school so that 'the notions of appropriate behaviour for each sex [are] converted into the appropriate academic disciplines'. In the familial environment, children develop gender-differentiated ideologies and behaviours. These do not necessarily have any direct relevance to school subjects such as French or physics. But new differentiations can be linked to existing ones, so that some school subjects come to be seen as masculine and others as feminine. This process is dialectical – there is a 'transference of femininity . . . from the student to the school subject and back again to the student' (MacDonald, 1980). Thus once a subject has acquired a masculine image, participation in it is seen to enhance a boy's masculinity and diminish a girl's feminity. MacDonald's discussion is purely theoretical and she does not provide any examples of the ways in which gender is re-contextualized in schools. However, this idea can fruitfully be applied to the question of the masculinity of science and discussion in this area can illustrate the more general point. [. . .]

One of the key components of adolescent masculinity is toughness. This takes many forms from physical rough and tumble to bravado and self-confidence and it is clearly evident in the science laboratory. Almost any piece of apparatus can be used or abused to demonstrate a boy's toughness, as these extracts from my field notes from the GIST project show.

> One example of force was a very strong magnet. Handed to boy to pass round, he and another boy immediately started a tug of war with it, only passed on at teacher's insistence. Periodically throughout lesson boys would try with it, girls never.

> Spring balance used as catapult (boys).

> Boys try to give each other shocks (with 6V battery!).

> One group [of boys] mimic an interrogation using ray box as a bright light.

This type of example could be multiplied endlessly. It happened in virtually every lesson where apparatus was used – which in the post-Nuffield era means virtually every science lesson.

Some apparatus really is potentially dangerous, and then boys' toughness may give them a real advantage. For example, in a chemistry lesson the pupils were heating a chemical and collecting the gas which was given off under water; there was a slight risk that the water could suck back into the test tube which might then crack and scatter its contents. The boys in the group commented 'great' when the teacher warned them of the danger, whereas the girls were obviously scared of the experiment. They approached it tentatively (which increased the danger) and panicked and squealed whenever a suck-back seemed imminent. The boys' greater confidence meant that their reaction to a potential suck-back was more positive – they heated the substance harder or took the tube out of the water. In the end several girls gave up their experiments and joined the boys' groups as onlookers.

Boys' toughness can take a verbal form. When one class were asked what they had thought of a test, the boys chorused 'easy' while the girls said rather plaintively that 'the electricity was horrible'. In fact, the boys and girls had done equally well on the test, so the difference in response was more indicative of attitude than achievement. To admit that they had had difficulty might have been seen as a sign of weakness in the boys.

The boys' self-confidence is also shown in the way they answer questions:

> . . . in class discussion round the front the boys were falling over themselves to give the answer and the girls were sitting back . . . Boys know technical vocabulary . . . Boys give lots of examples of light bending, mostly wrong (e.g. with magnet) but they don't care.

Here the boys are actively participating in the lesson, the girls are passively listening (or not listening). There is a considerable element of bravado in the boys' use of technical terms that they don't really understand, but if they don't mind taking the risk of being wrong there's always the chance that it will impress someone.

This enthusiastic participation by the boys left the girls at a considerable disadvantage, particularly over apparatus. The most striking instance of this was an incident observed by Barbara Smail. Pupils were doing an experiment in groups which involved heating carbohydrates over a flame. There were insufficient goggles for everyone, so the teacher stressed that only the person actually doing the heating should have a pair. When it was time to start the experiment all the boys rushed for the apparatus and grabbed the goggles. Soon nearly every boy in the class had a pair, with none left for the girls. Since pupils of this age always work in single sex groups by choice, the girls could not do the experiment. They had to go round the groups of boys begging for pairs of goggles – and generally getting short shrift until the teacher noticed what was happening and intervened. By the time the girls were properly equipped they were so behind with the experiment that they could not complete it before the end of the period, and so got very little out of the lesson – although they probably learned something about power relationships.

This is an extreme example, but similar situations are not uncommon. Boys frequently make a dash for the apparatus and end up with the lion's share, or at least the bits in better condition. Although this could be seen merely as an indication of boys' greater enthusiasm, it can also be interpreted in terms of male dominance. Whyte (1984) has described how boys push into queues ahead of girls, 'persuade' them to give up scarce pieces of apparatus and monopolize the classroom space. This is evident in science as elsewhere. For example:

Boys wanted to show teacher their completed table of results. Often pushed in on a demonstration. When girls wanted help they waited till teacher had finished whatever she was doing.

At one point a boy donned the goggles that a girl had put down for a second . . . the teacher noticed this and reprimanded him. he gave the goggles back, assuming surprise that she had not finished.

Rush for apparatus at start of practical – a crush of boys with a few girls, most girls followed later.

The boys . . . moved freely around the room, chatting to each other . . . the girls restricted themselves to their benches and the teacher's table.

Boys act as though they have automatic priority over the resources of the laboratory, whether they be the apparatus, the teacher's attention, or just the physical space. One of the general principles of a patriarchal society – that males are more important than females – is acted out in the science classroom in a way which limits girls' opportunities to learn.

Boys' assumption of their own superiority can also be seen in their interactions with girls in class. [. . .] It was not uncommon for a boy to shout out the answer to a question directed at a girl before she had a chance to answer. Boys seemed to think they knew more about science than the girls and they tried to demonstrate their superiority. For example, I noted,

one boy cruises round inspecting girls' written work almost like a teacher.

boys outside look at girls' work through window, make comments.

and sometimes the girls acquiesced:

several occasions on which girls watch boys doing experiments, as if to learn from them.

However, classroom interactions were not always as amicable as this. Adolescent boys are characteristically scornful of girls, and there were many instances of boys using ridicule to remind the girls of their inferior status.

when girls ask questions in class discussion, boys tend to groan (3 times). [Teacher] controls them, 'no it's a good question'.

quite a lot of put-down comments from boys to girls. Jane has already done today's work . . . and complains about doing it again. Boys call out, 'you're stupid though, aren't you, Jane'.

Girl: 'I got it wrong' (spelling)
Boy: 'You would do, wouldn't you?'

There are no examples in the notes of this sort of comment directed at boys by girls. [. . .]

So far I have been concentrating on boys and the way their masculine behaviour, when imported into the laboratory, helps to establish science as a male domain. But boys' behaviour is only part of the picture. Girls' feminine traits also have a role to play. For example, girls' timidity may mean that they take less part in classroom discussions and avoid experiments which they consider dangerous. It also tends to make them fearful of venturing into new ground. This was illustrated in a lesson where the children were supposed to weigh a few things of their own when they had completed their worksheets: whereas the boys measured a great variety of objects, the girls tended to sit around doing nothing or repeated their previous measurements. In this and other experiments the girls checked with each other and with the boys that they had got the right answer.

Low self-confidence is linked to conscientiousness as pupils try to ensure that they are doing the correct thing. Teachers frequently remark that girls are more conscientious than boys and this was certainly evident in the science laboratories. Sometimes it stood the girls in good stead – they were more likely to be working than the boys who tended to play around with their apparatus the moment the teacher's back was turned (often to the annoyance of the girls). But sometimes it backfired. School science equipment is rough and ready and does not lend itself to precise measurement. In a lesson where pupils had to balance a ruler on a sharp edge by moving weights to different positions, the girls got worried if the ruler was not completely level and spent a long time trying to achieve perfect equilibrium. Because of this they did not experiment with many different positions of the weights; the boys' less precise approach meant that they quickly built up a table of results from which they could work out the general principles.

Of course some girls *are* good at science. But even they seem to realize that their success is not somthing to brag about. In a lesson on heat there were two girls, Jean and Helen, who obviously understood what was going on and handled the technical vocabulary with ease. Towards the end of the lesson the pupils had to write up the experiment, explaining the pattern they got on their graphs. A group of girls called out to Jean, asking her what to say. She replied, 'I don't know, I'll manage when I get home, I'll ask my Dad' and then went to give them the correct explanation. She was then called over by a group of boys and was explaining the work to them until the teacher sent her back to her seat. Although Jean's ability was clearly recognized by the rest of the class, she herself played it down and attributed her knowledge to her Dad (not, of course, to her Mum).

It could be argued that Jean was taking the teacher's role here in the same way as the boys discussed earlier who inspected the girls' work. But the teacher in class acts both as helper and as judge of the pupils' work. In context it seemed that Jean was acting as a helper, called in where she was needed, whereas the boys were judging girls' work without being asked to do so. It was not unusual to see a group of girls being helped by a competent friend, but able boys were more likely to be working alone or competing with one other to see who could get through the worksheets fastest.

Another common sight was that of a girl acting as a helper to a boy. This again can be seen as a way in which familial gender roles are transformed at school. Girls are frequently socialized into a service role, providing for and tidying up after men, and they continue these tasks in the laboratory:

Boy (Nigel) on back bench has girls there working for him. They are getting on better with the experiment than he is, but he's definitely in charge. Pinches their light bulb, teases them with it. Girl helps him make his circuit work – he comments that hers (which is working) is wrong, and that he hasn't got the woman's touch. When they decide that his board is defective, Nigel sends girl to teacher with it. In cleaning up she again carries his board to put it away.

At one point a couple of boys moved their apparatus to a girls' table and girls helped them do it. After a short while the boys started using a ruler as a springboard to flip brass squares.

Four girls chosen. . . to give out workbooks.

At the end several girls were helping the teacher pack up the apparatus, count brass squares, etc. Other pupils were working on the arithmetical problems.

It does not take much insight to deduce that pupils who are working on arithmetical problems are learning a different lesson than those who are counting brass squares!

A strong component of femininity is concern with people. This can be difficult to manifest in science, where the brass squares, light bulbs and copper sulphate often seem to have nothing to do with people. Some girls solve this problem by focusing on the teacher rather than the subject matter. They manufacture opportunities for interaction with the teacher:

> Teacher wanders round room. Whenever he approaches girls' bench they seem to find something to ask . . . Boys more often ignore T's presence. Particularly noticeable with group of girls at front bench who chat to teacher whenever he sits to mark books, etc.

> At start of practical work several girls seemed to go to [teacher] with trivial questions about what to do. [Teacher]: 'What does it *tell* you to do?' They prefer instructions in personal form, rather than impersonally from worksheets.

> Some of the girls took a 'mothering' role, e.g. discussing boil on teacher's neck, advising him what to do about it. At other times he seemed to be almost flirting with them, discussing their English exam, their haircut, etc.

Although the freedom of movement and opportunities for conversation in the science lab do allow for inter-personal interaction this remains peripheral – or even antipathetic – to the science being taught. The masculine concern with things fits more easily with the dominant form of physical science than the feminine concern with people. This is much less true of biology and may be one of the reasons that biology has a feminine or neutral image.

Adolescent girls are generally greatly concerned about their looks. In every lesson I have observed one or more girls brushed or combed her hair. This is another aspect of femininity which can be at odds with science. For safety reasons hair is supposed to be tied back in laboratories and protective clothing sometimes has to be worn. None of this is glamorous and girls are often reluctant to comply:

> Teacher tells kids to wear safety goggles during practical, when girl asks why he replies 'you want to stay beautiful don't you?' I think this emphasis on beauty is counter-productive – safety goggles are anything but flattering and at later stages of the practical very few girls were actually wearing them – most propped up on their hair or lying on benches. No hair was tied back. Quite a lot of hairdressing (brushing, styling, etc.) during lesson.

In fact this reluctance to wear goggles seemed to be greatest in the class where the teacher (by his own admission) made a point of emphasizing the girls' femininity.

Many teachers, consciously or unconsciously, use gender stereotypes in their lessons. One head of science, reflecting on the experience of being observed in the GIST project, wrote that:

If no obvious interest in the subject or topic is displayed, the male teaching staff often flatter the girls or are mildly flirtatious towards them, finding that this is often a successful way of encouraging them. In the same circumstances male teachers will probably appeal to the boys' competitive instincts. We accept that treating the sexes differently in this way may well be encouraging them to see their roles in the world of science differently but are reluctant to abandon successful teaching techniques.

Here a 'successful teaching technique' seems to mean one that makes the lesson happen rather than one which develops in girls a lasting interest in science. He continues:

It is less acceptable (isn't it?) for women teachers to flirt with pupils and few do. However, they too fall into the trap of appealing to competitiveness or bravado in the boys. To get the girls moving a commonly used appeal is 'Don't let the boys show us girls up!'

We did not observe any incidents which manifested the sort of feminine solidarity between teacher and pupils suggested by the last sentence. However, there were certainly examples of teachers who appealed to male bravado. One of the clearest cases occurred in a discussion between a male head of chemistry in a mixed school and a female head of chemistry from a girls' school. The man described how he conducted the common experiment in which coal dust is mixed with water and then filtered out so that clean water emerges from the black sludge. He commented that he always dared his class to drink the water; the boys usually did, but the girls hung back. He concluded from this that the girls were in some way inadequate in science – and presumably the girls reached a similar conclusion. However, the woman teacher replied that when she did the same experiment she mixed some colouring with the water before filtering, so that a pretty pink liquid appeared at the end. By so doing she was appealing to the girls' aesthetic sense where the male teacher was utilizing the boys' bravado. The science was the same (except that the girls learned that only some impurities are removed by filtering – the colouring remained) but the context was masculine in one case and feminine in the other.

Another way in which teachers' pre-conceptions may influence their relationship with girls and boys is in their perception of who is competent and who needs help. Crossman (1981) has shown that science teachers (like teachers of other subjects (Spender, 1982)) generally interact more with boys than with girls in class. With the GIST teachers, who knew what we were interested in, we did not find any differences in the overall number of interactions with girls and with boys (Whyte, 1984). However, there was a tendency for the interactions to be of a different nature. This was most obvious in a lesson taken by a probationary teacher where I noted that

In the question and answer part of the lesson boys interacted with the teacher much more than girls. Boys were far more often picked to answer questions than girls, even when girls had their hands up. Girls were more tentative about volunteering, tended to put their hands up and down again. In the practical part of the lesson the teacher spent a lot more time helping the girls than the boys. In some cases he seemed to be setting the apparatus up for them rather than helping them do it themselves. At the end the boys were appealing, 'Sir, come and look at ours'. The distinct impression from this lesson was that the boys knew the answers and the girls couldn't do the practical.

This tendency for teachers to help the girls more than the boys was fairly common, but by no means universal.

Another common difference in the treatment of the sexes which does not show up in a simple count is that boys are often called on to give the correct answer when a girl has failed. For example:

> Teacher: 'Does anybody except David know what that means? Do you know Linda or Tracey at the back? Sharon you've been quiet. Go on David, tell them.'

This emphasizes that fact that the boy, David, is more knowledgeable than the three girls. It would probablay have been possible to find a girl in the class who *did* know, or to rephrase the question so that Linda, Tracey or Sharon could work it out. [. . .]

However, I do not want to exaggerate the teacher's part in maintaining gender differentiation. On the contrary it is my contention that it is largely the behaviour of the children themselves which is crucial. Boys bring with them to science lessons a conception of masculinity which includes toughness, aggression, activity and disdain for girls; girls bring with them a conception of femininity which includes timidity, conscientiousness, deference, person orientation and a concern for appearance. These self-definitions lead girls and boys to behave in different ways, such that boys come to dominate the laboratory and establish it as their territory. Gender differentiated behaviour outside school leads to gender differentiated behaviour in science lessons, which in turn leads to science acquiring a masculine image. The in-school and out-of-school behaviours are by no means identical, but they have a common source in children's gender identity. [. . .]

Inherent masculinity

The three arguments that I have discussed so far all hold, to a greater or lesser extent, that the masculinity of science is an *image*. Whether it is caused by textbook representations, by curriculum organization or by classroom behaviour, it is essentially a distortion of science. The word 'image' is closely linked to 'imaginary' and these three mechanisms all suggest that the masculinity of science is only an illusion, not an intrinsic part of its nature.

The final position is that science as it is currently practised is inherently masculine. Manthorpe (1982) has [. . .] summarized this view as the belief that

> The problem is more fundamental than the operation of a stereotype which alternative text-books and teaching attitudes can effectively counter. Rather the

assumption is that science is a social construct, its development is inextricably linked with social relations, not least the relations between men and women. Thus science in a patriarchal, or male-dominated society has in-built features which actively discourage girls and women from studying it.

These in-built features are the abstract, analytic, 'objective' and controlling nature of science, developed so that 'natural philosophers could . . . demonstrate their virility by the scientific and technological appropriation of a mechanical earth' (Easlea, 1981). Overfield (1981) argues that 'Woman . . . is only able to enter and pursue a scientific career by virtue of denying everything the scientific ethos says is woman's nature, or by becoming a surrogate man', while Keller (1983) suggests that 'our earliest experiences incline us to associate the affective and cognitive posture of objectification with masculine, while all processes which involve a blurring of the boundary between subject and object tend to be associated with the feminine'. [. . .]

Some proponents of the view that science is inherently masculine reject out of hand any question of working through the schools. Overfield (1981) says bluntly that 'This approach has never worked, and can never work, for it is based on a complete untruth. Science now is the embodiment of values currently esteemed as male and masculine . . . It is patently not a question of getting more girls to do scientific courses or of 'sexism' on the part of individuals or institutions'. Certainly at first sight the suggestion that science is inherently masculine appears radically different from the suggestion that science is packaged in a masculine way. But on closer inspection these views may converge. If school science were altered to be more girl-friendly, centred around girls' interests and ways of working, would this not be one step to creating a feminine science? And if considerable numbers of girls (and boys) emerged from school having learned science in this way, would science as an institution begin to change? This is not the place to take such speculations further, but it may be that this view of the masculinity of science is not as different from the first three as some of its proponents would have us believe. [. . .]

References

Crossman, M. (1981). *Sex differences and teacher/pupil interaction patterns in secondary school science*, M. Ed. Dissertation. Manchester University. See Chapter 7 in this volume.

Department of Education and Science (1983). *Statistics of Education 1982*. HMSO.

Easlea, B. (1981). *Science and Sexual Oppression*. Weidenfeld & Nicolson.

Gaetana, M.A.K. (1966). 'A study to determine the distribution of male and female figures in elementary science text books', *Journal of Research in Science Teaching*, Vol. 4, pp. 178–9.

Gilligan, C. (1982). *In a Different Voice*. Harvard University Press.

Heikkenen, H. (1978). 'Sex bias in chemistry texts: where is women's place?' *The Science Teacher*, Vol. 45, pp. 16–21.

Hilmo, I. (1983). 'An analysis of Norwegian textbooks in science'. Paper prepared for 2nd Girls and Science and Technology Conference, Norway.

Keller, E.F. (1983). 'Gender and science'. In Harding, S. and Hintikka, M.B. (eds), *Discovering Reality: feminist perspectives on epistomology, meta physics, methodology and the philosophy of science*. Reidel.

Kelly, A. (1976). 'Women in physics and physics education'. In Lewis, J. (ed.), *New Trends in Physics Teaching*, Vol. III, pp. 241–66. UNESCO.

Kelly, A. (1982). 'Science in Soviet Schools', *Women and Education Newsletter*, No. 24.

Kelly, A., Whyte, J. and Smail, B. (1984). *Final Report of the GIST Project*. Department of Sociology, University of Manchester. See Chapter 11, this volume.

Lensik, M. (1983). 'Girls, physics and technology in the Netherlands: the MENT project'. Paper prepared for 2nd Girls and Science and Technology Conference, Norway.

MacDonald, M. (1980). 'Schooling and the reproduction of class and gender relations'. In Barton, L., Meighan, R., and Walker, S. (Eds). *Schooling, Ideology and the Curriculum*. Falmer.

Manthorpe, C. (1982). 'Men's science, women's science or science? Some issues related to the study of girls' science education', *Studies in Science Education*, Vol. 9, pp. 65–80.

Overfield, K. (1981). 'Dirty fingers, grime and slag heaps: purity and the scientific ethic'. In Spender, D. (ed.), *Men's Studies Modified*. Pergamon.

Samuel, J. (1981). 'Experiences of teaching chemistry in a mixed comprehensive school'. In Kelly, A. (ed.), *The Missing Half: Girls and Science Education*. Manchester University Press.

Smail, B. (1984). *Girl-Friendly Science*. Schools Council/Longman. See Chapter 9, this volume.

Spender, D. (1982). 'The role of teachers: what choices do they have?' In Council of Europe (ed.), *Sex Stereotyping in Schools*. Swets & Zeitlinger.

Taylor, J. (1979). 'Sexist bias in physics textbooks', *Physics Education*, Vol. 13, pp. 227–80.

Walford, G. (1980). 'Sex bias in physics textbooks', *School Science Review*, Vol. 62, pp. 220–7.

Walford, G. (1981). 'Do chemistry textbooks present a sex-biased image?' *Education in Chemistry*, Vol. 18, pp. 18–19.

Walford, G. (1983). 'Science education and sexism in the Soviet Union', *School Science Review*, Vol. 64, pp. 213–24.

Whyte, J. (1984). 'Observing sex stereotypes and interactions in the school lab and workshop', *Educational Review*, Vol. 36, pp. 75–86.

Part III
Curriculum Content

9 Organizing the curriculum to fit girls' interests

Barbara Smail

The basic aims of science education between 11 and 16 have been defined by the Secondary Science Curriculum Review (SSCR, 1983). If these aims are translated into practice in schools, they should be successful in removing some of the sex imbalance in post-16 science classes. Science for all up to the end of the fifth year will move the point of choice away from early adolescence to an age when more mature decisions can be made. The inclusion in the aims of SSCR of statements such as the following suggest that the new curriculum will emphasize the human and social implications of science.

> . . . the Review will initiate development work that enables schools to provide, at appropriate stages of a five-year programme, adequate opportunities for all students to
>
> study those aspects of science that are essential to an understanding of oneself, and of one's personal well-being;
>
> study key concepts that are essential to an understanding of the part science and technology play in a post-industrial and technological society;
>
> appreciate that technologies are expressions of the desire to understand and control the environment and that technologies change in response to changing social needs.

This bias should appeal to girls since Ormerod (1981) has shown that girls who had a positive view of the effects of science on the environment and the human race were more likely to choose physical science. For boys, there was no relationship between such favourable views and choice of physics and chemistry; however, an understanding of the practical value of science to the individual correlated significantly with choosing physical science for boys but not for girls. Thus girls who choose science may have altruistic motives, whereas, for boys, the choice may be largely instrumental, opening up career possibilities.

Source: Chapter 4 of Girl-Friendly Science Schools Counil/Longman, 1984.

Table 1. Most popular topics for 11-year-old girls and boys on entry to secondary school (percentage of children responding 'I'd like to know more')

Girls		Boys	
	per cent		per cent
1. What food is good for you	73 (56)	1. How motor cars work	78 (30)
2. How children develop	70 (52)	2. Computers	73 (47)
3. Our eyes and how we see	65 (51)	3. Volcanoes and earthquakes	71 (48)
4. What makes a rainbow appear	63 (47)	4. Stars and planets	71 (46)
5. How a record is made	63 (60)	5. How machines work	67 (26)
6. Germs and illnesses	60 (36)	6. How transistor radios work	66 (31)
7. Animals in the jungle	60 (60)	7. Nuclear power	64 (25)
8. Our ears and how we hear	58 (41)	8. Acids and chemicals	63 (56)
9. How our muscles work	58 (59)	9. How a record is made	60 (63)
10. Acids and chemicals	56 (63)	10. Animals in the jungle	60 (60)

The figure in brackets is the percentage of the other sex answering 'I'd like to know more'.

Other research (Bottomley and Ormerod, 1977) suggests that girls like biology best when it is nurturative – caring for plants and animals – rather than analytical. There is also some suggestion from the labelling of topics 'boys' science' and 'girls' science' by children (Ebbutt, 1981) that the science girls like is aesthetic and has an end-product, e.g. extracting plant scents, chromatography and making crystals, whereas 'boys' science' involves developing rules from observations in work on elements, electrical circuits, air pressure etc.

When the children taking part in the Girls into Science and Technology (GIST) project[1] were asked to indicate their interest in finding out more about certain science topics there were marked sex differences, as shown in Table 1. The overwhelming emphasis on the human body for girls and machines for boys is obvious. However, many boys are also interested in human biology. Acids and chemicals, how a record is made, and animals in the jungle are equally appealing to both sexes. Girls' interest in rainbow fits the idea that aesthetics is part of 'girls' science' (Ebbutt, 1981), while boys' interest in volcanoes and earthquakes, stars and planets and nuclear power suggests a concern with large and powerful forces.

Personality and interest in science

A recent book by Carol Gilligan (1982) on the development of the sense of moral values in girls and boys draws together some ideas about masculine and feminine personality and role development which may be relevant to the sex split in science interest. Chodorow (1974) argues from a psycho-analytic perspective that, since women are largely responsible for early child care, early experiences of individuation and relationship are different for girls and boys. This means that girls emerge from early childhood with a basis for empathy built into their primary definition of self. Boys' development necessitates a more complete separation from mother and hence male personality defines itself less in terms of relation to other people than does female personality. Gilligan re-examines several studies in the light of Chodorow's hypothesis, arguing that psychology in the past has interpreted this lack of separation in women as female inferiority, whereas, considered from the point of view of groups of people co-existing, it presents an equally valid and, in some cases, superior way of looking at the world. A brief review of Gilligan's re-analysis of the work of Lever, Piaget, Kohlberg and Erikson illustrates how she develops her thesis.

Lever (1976) studied the organization and structure of play activities among 181 children of between 10 and 11. She reported large sex differences in behaviour. The boys play in larger and more age-heterogeneous groups. They play more competitive games and they do not terminate a game if a quarrel occurs. They develop a complicated system of rules to deal with the situation. Girls, on the other hand, play in small groups with friends close to their own age. Disagreements occur less frequently than for boys but, when they do, the game is abandoned. Piaget (1968) also noticed boys becoming increasingly fascinated by the legal elaboration of rules and development of fair procedures for adjudicating conflicts. Girls, Piaget observed, have a more pragmatic attitude towards rules 'regarding a rule as good as long as the game repaid it'. Girls are more tolerant in their attitudes towards rules, more willing to make exceptions and more easily reconciled to innovation. Piaget interpreted this as a lack of legal sense among girls. Lever also implied that girls' sensitivity and care for the feelings of others has little market value in a society based on modern corporate success. Her observations suggest that girls subordinate the continuation of the game to the relationship.

Kohlberg (1981) saw six stages in the moral development of the child. Stages 5 and 6 are defined in terms of ability to apply universal principles of justice. At stage 4, the developing adult is able to see *relationships* as *subordinate to rules*. Kohlberg developed his theory on the basis of a study of 84 boys over a 20-year period. When his theory was tested on women they scored only at stage 3 since they tended to see each problem in context and linked to the people in the situation rather than abstracted. Gilligan argues that Piaget and Kohlberg are applying men's conception of morality as *fairness* tied to understanding of *rights and rules*. She suggests that women's conception of morality, as concerned with the activity of care, bases moral development on the understanding of *responsibility and relationships*. Within Kohlberg's system, women fail to develop beyond stage 3 because they construct the moral problem differently to men.

In her own study of college students Gilligan found women more likely to define themselves in terms of a network of relationships. Their positive view of themselves was linked to a judgement of their capacity for caring. For men in the study, great ideas or distinctive activity was the standard against which they assessed themselves and their success. While women saw the world as networks of relationships, men saw it in terms of hierarchies.

Using Erikson's (1963) model of psychosocial development as a basis, Gilligan implies that whereas for boys the task of adolescence is the forging of an identity by separation, for girls it is the achievement of intimacy through relationships. From identity, boys move towards intimacy and relationship; girls in general attain identity *after* intimacy. It can be argued that girls and boys approaching adolescence have different concerns and therefore different interests in science. Boys are concerned with making sense of the world through rules, and achieving an individual identity; they aspire to a position in an hierarchy. Girls' concerns centre on developing a network of close relationships with other people. They interpret the world through its effects on these relationships and do not abstract events from their context as readily.

Given that girls and boys are so different by the age of 11, to teach the same science in the same laboratory, and make it interesting to both sexes, seems an impossibility!

Curriculum modification

From our findings in the initial survey and the work of others described above, we on the GIST project had a number of ideas about making science more appealing to girls. I have formalized these ideas in Table 2 below. There is no clear distinction between boys and girls in the characteristics in Table 2.

Table 2. Characteristics of children and science education

Analytical/Instrumental	Nurturative
Interest in rules	Interest in relationships
Interest in machines	Interest in people
Interest in fairness and justice	Pragmatism
Views world as hierarchy of relationships (competitive)	Views world as network of relationships (co-operative)
Emphasis on analytical thought	Emphasis on aesthetic appreciation
Interest in controlling inanimate things	Interest in nurturing living things

Undoubtedly some girls enjoy analysing situations, applying rules and controlling machines, just as some boys enjoy caring for living things and appreciate the beauty of the world around them. Each pair of characteristics represents the extremes of a scale, and individuals would be placed at various points on each of the six scales. However, the evidence of sex differences in interests suggests two overlapping distributions, with more girls on the nurturative side of the scale and more boys on the analytical/instrumental side.

The position of school science curricula on similar scales will vary from school to school according to the interests, personalities and previous experience of the staff within the school. In GIST, we attempted to make science more easily accessible to girls by reducing emphasis on the characteristics on the left of the table, and emphasizing those on the right. [. . .]

Rules v. relationships

One task undertaken early in the project was the re-organization of the *Insight to Science* Environment Unit (ILEA, 1979). This unit consisted of a series of 20 work cards describing experiments on building materials and animals' homes, air and water pollution, the inter-relationship of living things and colonies of bacteria. Staff using this unit in one school complained that it did not work as a series of independent work cards, from which the children were supposed to deduce a number of ideas about the environment and its preservation; the links between one experiment and the next needed explanation and amplification if the children were to gain anything from the exercise. The 20 work card experiments were, therefore, re-organized around the themes of Homes, Air, Water and Soil. Additional descriptive material was added to the original experiments to emphasize the importance to human life of a clean environment, and the part played by women like Rachel Carson in raising public awareness of the problem of pollution. These adaptations drastically altered the emphasis and the style of the science lessons. The original unit had consisted of a string of experiments linked by rather abstract ideas or rules, and the children were supposed to do the experiments individually or in small groups to work out what was happening and why. This produced a lot of competition to see who could get all the right answers and finish the unit first. The new material seemed to generate a more genuine interest among both boys and girls in the content being studied, because the experiments were set firmly in context. The teacher was able to adopt a more questioning, less omniscient style, and class discussions about environmental issues arose spontaneously.

This example illustrates a shift from a 'masculine' approach to science centring on the development of a system of rules for measuring the levels of air and water pollution to science with a more feminine outlook, which stresses a concern for people and animals and sees *caring* for the environment as more important than *analysing* how far the damage has gone. I must stress, at this point, that all the experiments from the original work cards were retained in the modified scheme. I am not advocating the total abandonment of analysis in favour of pure description, but, rather that the science 'skeleton' should have much more flesh on its bones! For girls, the context is very important and experiments need to be interspersed with more explanatory discussions, reading and written work, so that a synthesis of 'male' and 'female' characteristics is achieved.

Controlling the inanimate while nurturing the living

In many project schools, there was a ready acceptance of the idea of linking physics principles to human biology whenever possible. In one school, we developed a first-year booklet on Lungs and Air Pressure. A pocket spirometer was used to measure each child's lung capacity. They also measured their lung pressure using a giant water manometer. This led to a discussion of diseases of the lungs and a film about the danger of smoking. Several schools have tried approaching a systematic study of light from the desire to understand how the human eye works. A visiting woman scientist who was an anatomy lecturer, helped children find the muscles, bones and nerves in their arms when studying forces, levers and pivots. These connections have been made before in printed schemes. Our innovation was to put the application first, before any theory, rather than studying light or forces in an abstract sense, with the practical application at the end of the topic.

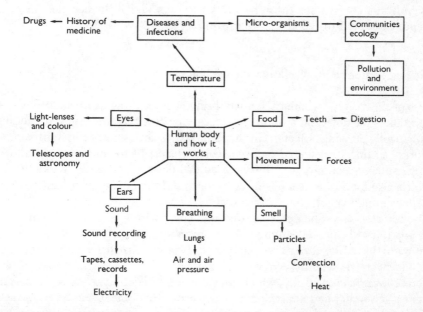

Figure 1.   Map of a lower school science curriculum based on the human body.

A network of connections between physical science and human biology topics is shown in Figure 1. Although none of the GIST schools went this far, it would be possible to build up a lower school science curriculum on this basis.

Wherever relevance to home life could be spelled out, girls' interest was captured. A unit of work on electricity for one school started by considering a world without electricity. Investigations of record players and tape-recorders led to ideas about circuits. A model electric blanket was made and used to demonstrate principles of electrical safety in the home (based on Darrall, 1980).

In designing their talks, a number of the visiting women scientists made use of girls' interest in making machines safe for people. A polymer technologist showed how she tested plastics for use in making crash-helmets or building chemical plants. A physicist working for the Factory Inspectorate showed how air samples were filtered to check the level of asbestos fibres and dust and to ensure safe working conditions.

When written curriculum materials in use in the GIST schools were examined for sex bias, we noticed a tendency for some teachers to emphasize the danger of science, particularly electricity, sometimes in a rather humorous way. One workbook cover featured Frankenstein's monster wired to large discharge tubes and surrounded by sparks. A set of instructions for building small electronics devices began with a list of six statements in block capitals beginning 'DO NOT'. We felt that these materials probably appealed to male bravado but might discourage more timid girls from taking part. [. . .] There are numerous occasions in the early years of science when teachers can choose where they put the emphasis: do they praise the loudest 'pops' when children are making hydrogen or the most beautiful hydrogen soap bubbles? These seemingly insignificant choices set the tone of the lessons and influence the image of science presented to the class as harmful or caring.

Bringing aesthetic appreciation into science

Most of the visiting women scientists brought interesting samples to illustrate their talks. We noted on a number of occasions how the girls enjoyed handling aesthetically pleasing objects. This happened with such widely different samples as brass castings, preserved embryo seals, whales' teeth, mounted metallurgy samples, hand-made wooden boxes in animal designs and geology samples.

Girls also found the marvels of astronomy and the beauty of the microscopic world exciting. An astronomer talked about why the sky is blue and why the sun turns red as it sets. She demonstrated this effect with a tank of water in which she precipitated colloidal sulphur. An electron microscopist showed how crystal size was affected by formation conditions. It is curious that many of the most notable women scientists have worked in the fields of astronomy and microscopy/crystallography, which combine aesthetic observation with analysis. A sense of wonder and appreciation of scientific phenomena can be encouraged by incorporating more imaginative writing exercises into science lessons. The first year pupils who did the lungs and air pressure unit, particularly enjoyed writing letters 'from Pascal' describing his experiments with barometers at sea level and on mountain peaks.

Harding (1979) has suggested that girls perform better on essay questions, boys on multiple-choice questions, and that structured items might be fairer. [. . .] Multiple-choice assessment often tests recall rather than understanding and higher thinking processes. It could be argued that it reinforces the view of science as a subject concerned only with learning and regurgitating facts. A move away from multiple-choice exercises to structured and essay style homework and tests in the early years would develop both girls' and boys' understanding of work done in lessons by requiring them to organize their ideas for themselves, instead of accepting 'conventional wisdom'. Since girls are slightly favoured by this form of assessment, the results might build their confidence in their ability to succeed at science. Using this reasoning, one GIST school made use of the following list of ideas for devising extended writing homework exercises and examination questions:

Instructions (e.g. to a younger child) on how to make something, such as an electric motor.

Descriptions of solutions to problems in unusual situations (e.g. building a distillation apparatus from bits and pieces available on a desert island).

Letters to friends describing experiments or concepts.

Letters to newspapers expressing ideas on social implications of science (e.g. dumping of nuclear waste, seal-culling, vivisection).

Newspaper reports (e.g. of acid tanker accident, hazards and clean-up).

Advertisements (e.g. for Bunsen burners and other laboratory equipment).

Imaginative accounts (e.g. carbon or nitrogen cycle from the point of view of an atom involved, expeditions into ears, blood stream).

Diaries.

Script for TV interviews of inventors (e.g. *Tomorrow's World* describes a new advance in clinical thermometers. Some of these could then be acted out by the class)

Poems on scientific phenomena.

Extended answers also allow pupils to develop the context in which a scientific idea is useful, rather than remembering it in isolation. A less rigorously conceptual, more applied science approach in schools makes sense for both girls and boys. The Nuffield schemes from which much of present day British science teaching derives were intended to build up a systematic body of knowledge for future science specialists. Most children in British schools today are unlikely to become practising research scientists, but do need to know about how science affects their lives. Science courses in which there is less emphasis on acquiring factual knowledge and skills, and in which some time is spent discussing scientific issues and values, would benefit both specialist and non-specialist students.

Guidelines for developing a girl-friendly science curriculum

(a) Set experiments in context by providing background information about the possible uses and applications of scientific principles. Do this, if possible, before the ideas are derived by experiment – tell the pupils where they are going and why.
(b) Link physical science principles to the human body.
(c) Stress safety precautions rather than dangers.
(d) Discuss scientific issues, e.g. the microprocessor revolution and unemployment, energy and the bomb, aiming at a balanced view of the benefits and disadvantages of scientific developments.
(e) Make aesthetically appealing exhibitions.
(f) Use imaginative writing as an aid to assimilating scientific principles and ideas.

Notes

1. See Chapter 11 in this volume.

References

Bottomley, J.M. and Ormerod, M.B. (1977). 'Middle school science activities and their association with liking for science', *Education in Science*, No. 74, p. 23.
Chodorow, N. (1974). 'Family structures and feminine personality'. In Rosaldo, M.Z. and Lamphere, L. (eds), *Women, Culture and Society*. Stanford University Press.
Darall, F.L. *et al* (1980). *Open Science*. Hart-Davis Educational and Hutchinson Educational.
Ebbutt, D. (1981). 'Girls' science: boys' science revisited'. In Kelly, A. (ed.), *The Missing Half: Girls and Science Education*. Manchester University Press
Erikson, E.H. (1963). *Childhood and Society*. W.W. Norton.
Gilligan, C. (1982). *In a Different Voice*. Harvard University Press.
Harding, J. (1979). 'Sex differences in examination performance at 16+', *Physics Education*, Vol. 14, pp. 280–4.
ILEA (1979). *Insight to Science*. Addison-Wesley.
Kohlberg, L. (1981). *The Philosophy of Moral Development, Moral Stages and the Idea of Justice*. Harper & Row.
Lever, J. (1976). 'Sex Differences in the Games Children Play', *Social Problems*, Vol. 23, pp. 478–487.
Ormerod, M.B. (1981). 'Factors differentially affecting the science subject preferences, choices and attitudes of girls and boys'. In Kelly, A. (ed.), *The Missing Half: Girls and Science Education*. Manchester University Press.
Piaget, J. (1968). *The Moral Judgement of the Child*. Routledge & Kegan Paul.
SSCR (1983). *Science Education 11–16: proposals for action and consultation*. Secondary Science Curriculum Review.

10 Courting the Positive Virtues: a Case for Feminist Science

Di Bentley and Mike Watts

Introduction

Normal, formal science is masculine. As Mitroff and Kilmann (1978) say:

> Conventional science is strongly masculine in its orientation, reflecting traditional stereotypical male values: it is 'hardnosed', objective, value-free; it eschews the ambiguous, the speculative, the vague, the beautiful and the good.

From a Kuhnian point of view, normal science is the paradigm that prevails before the advent of a revolutionary one. In this paper we speculate on the change of thinking and action that is required for a paradigmatic revolution to take place, from a masculine to a feminist view of science. However, our purpose in this paper is not to focus entirely upon science but to look instead at 'school science'. [. . .]

The question this raises might be: quite what a relevant and available science for girls would look like? What would that special provision be? How far should it go in changing the very nature of science itself? We suggest there are three current answers, each at a different stage of articulation. The first is *girl-friendly* science, the second is *feminine* science, and the third is *feminist* science. In this paper we consider each of these in turn and examine its virtues and drawbacks. Since our primary interest lies in articulating the third more fully, we spend rather more space on this than on the other two. We do so from a distinctive point of view, from a perspective entailing a 'particular humanist' model of science. We then consider some of the implications for science teachers and curriculum developers before briefly summarizing our arguments.

Girl-friendly science

The clearest case for girl-friendly science has been developed by Smail (1984) and Harding (1985). It is, in Smail's words, 'a compensatory approach'. School

Source: *European Journal of Science Education*, 1986, Vol. 8, pp. 121–134.

science is a masculine pursuit and the enactment of girl-friendliness is to flavour the proceedings to give it an enhanced appeal to girls. It is a case of providing a spoonful of sugar to help the medicine go down. The approach is pragmatically based, evolving from experiences within the Girls into Science and Technolgoy (GIST) project (Kelly *et al*, 1986). Smail describes, for example, a lunch-time 'girls-only' science club designed to build girls' confidence in handling tools and apparatus.

> Most of the staff picked stereotyped feminine activities, such as bread baking or crystal growing, to encourage the girls to come along to the first meetings, and changed to science projects with more 'masculine' associations, such as building electronics circuits, once girls' confidence had been gained. If the 'femininity' of the club was not stressed at the beginning, the girls were reluctant to join.

Thus, by modifying the image by which science is portrayed, it is possible to attract girls into the mainstream of scientific activities.[1] [. . .]

The essence of these approaches, as advocated by Smail and Harding, is to induce girls into a science that is essentially unchanged. Science remains the same – a masculine arena. School management techniques and classroom activities are designed within that in order to give girls a 'fair deal'. Smail says 'in adapting science to more "feminine" contexts, care must be taken to ensure that both sexes understand the same underlying scientific principles and can, *ultimately, abstract them from the context and apply them in other circumstances*' (our emphasis). For us, however, 'girl-friendliness' is a superficial ploy that studiously avoids some of the main problems. Before engaging more fully in that argument, though, we consider 'feminine' science.

Feminine science

Whilst Smail and Harding would not disagree with the analysis of science, or school science, as a masculine subject, it would seem to us that their recommendations for change seldom really broach the essence of the issue – the very masculinity of science. Both writers do make some moves in the direction of what we would call *feminine science*, particularly when discussing examples of classroom activities that emphasize so-operation and collaborative work embedded in a relevant social context (rather than some 'rather abstract ideas or rules'). [. . .]

Manthorpe (1982) has gone further. She states that a feminine view of science should be one that features:

> a holistic view in which social ethical and moral questions are unquestionably involved;
>
> a scientific community based on co-operation;
>
> respect for and equal valuation of different form of knowledge – including the irrational and the subjective.

placing emphasis on a re-writing of the intellect and emotion;
a revaluation of the belief that the quality of life has priority over economics.

Two aspects are worth drawing out of what she says. The first concerns the point about the re-unification of the cognitive and the affective. Manthorpe's statements begin to paint a different picture of science, where feelings about the issues involved should not and indeed *cannot* be divorced from the investigation taking place.

Her second theme, that of the different view that women have of relationships – the way that scientists co-operate – is also important and is taken up by other writers. For instance, Gilligan (1982) feels that feminine views of relationships are based upon hierarchies (a very masculine approach) but upon webs:

> the power of the images of hierarchy and web, their evocation of feelings, signifies the embeddedness of both of these images in the cycle of human life. The experiences of inequality and interconnection then give rise to the ethics of justice and care, the ideals of human relationship – the vision that self and others will be treated as of equal worth, that despite differences in power, things will be fair; the vision that everyone will be responded to and included, that no-one will be left alone and hurt.

[. . .] The dominant *image* of science is one of competition – of scientists driving to be 'first' with the most ideal or correct solution, of challenge and repudiation. The two views outlined above hold a vision of pupils being encouraged into a science education which makes much of feelings and engagement with issues, and with co-operation in working groups. In such groups, ideas would be welcomed because people have the courage and commitment to put them forward, and would not be evaluated and then dismissed by other individuals almost as a matter of course. The ambience would be one of caring, not overt competition.

This is 'feminine science education', in which the classroom atmosphere is one of a caring supportive web of relationships. This is, for us, significantly different to simply 'easing' the content of the curriculum into a shape whereby girls could feel more at home with it. However, we feel that there is still a further stage in the feminization of science education.

Feminist science

Girl-friendliness describes changing both the images and the stereotypes that science materials present; 'feminine' advocates a change in the atmospheres of lessons to encourage the notions of giving value to the ideas of others, and considering science in social and political contexts. In this section we break with the format we have adopted so far – of developing a case from what happens, or might happen, in science education – and look instead at science itself. [. . .] Whilst we do not attempt to construct feminist science *ab initio*, we do hope to develop the argument along a distinctive route. The picture we paint of feminist science is *particularly humanistic*, a term used by Mitroff and Kilmann (1981).

Later, we use this to argue for a change in both the context and substance of science education. In all, we are reviewing the nature of science:

> Revision – the act of looking back, of seeing with fresh eyes, of entering an old text from a new direction – is more for us than a chapter in cultural history: it is an act of survival. Until we can understand the assumptions in which we are drenched we cannot know ourselves. And this drive to self-knowledge, for woman, is more than a search for identity: it is a part of her refusal of the self-destructiveness of the male-dominated society.

This quote from Rich (1972) begins to describe feminist science. Unlike girl friendly and feminist *school science*, it is a re-vision, of the very investigative nature of science itself. We would maintain that feminist science is significantly different from traditional science in four main ways:

the views that it has of persons in science;

the nature of objectivity in scientific investigations;

what constitutes evidence and the nature of its collection and evaluation;

the views it has of the status of scientific knowledge.

These issues are not in themselves new; each has been tackled independently by a variety of authors over time. Considered together, as a whole, they represent a particular view of science neatly summarized by Mitroff and Kilmann (1981). They describe four types of scientist, the last – the 'particular humanist' – is described as being the most feminine. For the particular humanist, science is a personal, value-constituted, interested, partisan activity which is poetic, political action-oriented, a-causal and non-rational. Particular humanists prefer the logic of the unique and the singular, and are interested, 'all-too-human', biased and poetic characters, who are committed to the postulates of action-oriented science. Such scientists prefer modes of inquiry such as case studies and detailed in-depth, subjectively involved studies of particular events and individuals. A particular humanist does not see science as occupying a specialist position as a field of knowledge; rather, it may often be subordinate to older, more mystical forms of knowledge, such as poetry, literature, and art.

Our four main points above have been highlighted separately by different authors. The first point, an intensely personal approach to science, is one developed for example, by Polanyi (1964) and Maxwell (1984). Maxwell argues (as characteristic of his own Kuhnian scientific revolution) for a radical shift from a 'philosophy of knowledge' to a 'philosophy of wisdom'.

> The central and basic intellectual task of rational (scientific) inquiry, according to the philosophy of wisdom, is to help imbue personal and social lives with vividly imagined and criticized possible *actions* so that we may discover, and perform where possible, those actions which enable us to realize what is of value – happiness, health, sanity, beauty, friendship, love, freedom, justice, prosperity, joy, democracy, creative endeavour, co-operation and productive work.

He adds that knowledge and understanding can in themselves be valuable and that they are vital dimensions to almost all that is of value in life. But his emphasis is upon *personal* understanding – personal endeavours to see, to inquire into what is of value in the existence we live – pure inquiry . . . at its most fundamental and important:

> According to the philosophy of wisdom, the whole raison d'être of academic enquiry, from a purely intellectual standpoint, is to promote and aid personal inquiry pursued for its own sake, as an integral part of life. According to this view, even an academic discipline as apparently remote from human concerns as consmology, has a profoundly personal, social and creative aim: to enable people to improve their own personal knowledge and understanding of this cosmos in which we live.

A feminist science would see the philosophy of wisdom as being entirely congruent with views of the purposes of science. The enrichment of the quality of human life and the concern for individual development are aspects of science that a feminist viewpoint would wish to draw out.

The second point, the separation of the objective nature of scientific enquiry from the more subjective nature of feminine endeavours, is supported by the writings of Callaway (1981), MacKinnon (1982) and Keller (1983). Keller advocates a new perspective in scientific methodology by embracing (rather than rejecting) subjectivity. She says that

> [envisaging] science as personal . . . adds to our thinking about science the kind of thinking that is often said to be 'just like a woman'. The unique contribution feminism makes to more traditional studies of science is the use of that expertise that has traditionally belonged to women – not simply as a woman's perspective – but as a critical instrument.

MacKinnon sharpens this argument by rejecting the idea that the domain of woman-as-scientist is *just* subjective, partial and undetermined. Rather, such feminist constructs can, by their use, engender a critique of the so-called generality, disinterested and universally applicable methods used by masculine science. [. . .] From this point of view, then, feminist science creates an investigative paradigm in which feminine logic is the starting point, and subjectivity an integral and essential part. [. . .] In scientific enquiry of this nature, understanding is not achieved by remaining outside events and being objectively detached. Rather, it *can only* be achieved by including the event or object and becoming a part of it.

This leads to our third issue. School science portrays a picture of both the positivist and reductionist tradition of scientific methodology. [. . .] Positivistic science portrays theories as logically ordered sets of laws which explain reality. Arguably, such theories are examples of masculine logic and explain the reality of masculine science. Both the reality and the logic of women is often different to this, and given the opportunity to observe the same events, women may well advance theories that differ. Furthermore, they may look for confirmation of their theories in exactly those aspects of processes that males choose to dismiss.

Gilligan (1982) draws out something of the same argument when she examines ideas women hold about the role of rules in reality. She points out that women's reality is different and thus they look for different aspects of a situation before beginning to explain it. Or as Polanyi (1964) says:

> Every interpretation of nature, whether scientific, non-scientific or anti-scientific is based upon some intuitive conception of the general nature of things . . . a potential discovery may be thought to attract the mind which will reveal it – inflaming the scientist with creative desire.

[. . .] Polanyi claims that the discovery of 'truth' in science uses the evidence of the senses merely as clues, transcends these experiences to embrace a reality beyond this and calls into question quite what is acceptable evidence in science. We would suggest that feminist science is unafraid to look for evidence and explanation beyond the immediate information of the senses. [. . .] Feminist science can take a much more holistic view of events. Natural systems and processes are not simply a collection of variables, but have a unity which present systems of 'evidence collection' and 'explanation by reduction to essential logic' disguises from our view. [. . .]

Finally, to return to Mitroff and Kilmann. The most masculine of their scientists hold that knowledge is synonymous with precision, accuracy and reliability. Any event that cannot be subjected to such precision is set aside as not worth knowing, or worse still, not capable of being known. Such a view gives science a privileged position vis-à-vis other knowledge. Because it claims to be value-free and disinterested, it can set itself apart from other forms of knowledge with sharp lines of definition. It becomes high in a hierarchical ordering of fields of knowledge which begin with the very precise. Further, because of its preciseness and claims to accuracy on the grounds of being free of human biases, it acquires a status far exceeding its potential to deliver such accurate and disinterested knowledge. It acquires the image and status of being the *only* representative of truth.

Our particular humanist, however, bases her scientific endeavours not on impersonal, dispassionate knowledge, but on a 'feeling science'. Her science would not have a privileged position over and above the status of other forms of knowledge. The humanizing of scientific enquiry lifts from it the restriction of being the most important and validated source of truth. It can no longer be seen as the sole representative of objective reality. Rather, science to a particular humanist is something that is one of many human endeavours equal, for example, to poetry, art, and music as representations of aspects of the world. It is as political, mystical and passionate as any other human activity, and is openly acknowledged as such.

Views like these are clearly at odds with traditional forms of science. As Manthorpe (1985) points out, from a feminist perspective, science, and particularly the 'hard' physical sciences, can no longer claim a neutral objectivity, but are themselves imbued with male bias. She says:

At its most radical, this feminist perspective questions the very possibility of scientific objectivity . . . Feminists have noted the congruity between the perceived dominant characteristics of science – its objectivity, its rationality, its disinterestedness – and the dominant male stereotype.

Discussion

[. . .] We have argued that 'girl-friendliness' and 'feminine' science are both steps along a route towards the goal above, but that they fall short in leaving untouched the very masculinity of the content and style of science. We see that 'feminist' science, following the four characteristics through which we have portrayed it, might have four major consequences for the practice of school science.

Schools science should be reshaped in terms of the views it has of people in science
Specifically, science teachers and curriculum developers, both male and female, need to re-examine their views of science and re-define the purposes of science education.

Our view is that girls are seeking a school science that is consistent with our outline of feminist science. Our evidence stems from studies such as Bentley (1984), Ebbutt and Watts (1985), GASAT (1985). These give some indication that girls have their own particular conceptions of science and science education, and that these views are somewhat different to the actuality commonly found in classrooms. Specifically, their *expectations* of science are different. For example, girls do *not* think that science is necessarily a set of right answers; they *do* think that science should be a study which helps to provide answers to the problems of society – so that the quality of the lives of people will be enhanced. It might be argued that girls are seldom explicitly taught that science is any other way. Nevertheless, it remains a dominant image of science that it is an impersonal pursuit of correct solutions – and girls seem to be rejecting that ethos. [. . .]

It is the case that any significant humanization and enculturalization of science would require a major *volte-face* for many science teachers. To present it as moral, social, aesthetic and emotional as Smail (1984) suggests, rather than a 'hard', entirely rational and logical subject, would need some considerable revision. Teachers in turn will require some shift from curriculum developers to assist in the work of generating and developing materials suitable to capturing such issues.

School science should be recast in terms of its portryal of the nature of objectivity in scientific investigations
Specifically, teachers and curriculum developers must begin to view science, and its social implications, as the personal development of understandings of the world and the context of the people who inhabit it.

That is, teachers must stop viewing science education as solely the objective and dispassionate study of the world around us. This raises two main points. If girls are to be able to bring their personal and affective experiences to bear *within* the classroom, then they must be able to see how these fit with the science that is being taught. Where science is seen as a male domain, as coldly logical and disinterested, as female inappropriate, then this sharing of experince is unlikely to take place. To make science meaningful, science teachers must personalize and carefully contextualize science itself, whilst invoking and accepting the previous experiences and prior knowledge that girls bring to lessons. Clearly peer group activity, media presentations and everyday situations (amongst many other factors) influence girls' perceptions of science and scientific activity. One implication of recognizing that such influences are important is to take them seriously and use class time to explore the images of science and its limitations as an explanation of the human condition. Secondly, science must be seen as actionable *outside* the classroom in a way that fits with the social emancipation of groups and individuals. If science cannot be seen to be useful in the amelioration of human plight then, for girls, it loses point and purpose. School science, then, must go beyond classroom walls into the real problems of the outside community where it confronts and deals with social and political values.

An important feature of learning concerns an individual's perceptions of her own change. That is, how well she perceived that she is in tune with the medium and the message of science lessons. One implication of this might be that assessment techniques should contain a greater element of self-assessment by girls – which is valued and taken into account by teachers. If girls are to undergo conceptual, skills-based and/or attitudinal changes then self-evaluation of their own change in performance is important. It is reinforcement – by their own measure – that science and their understanding of it has meaning.

School science must be revisited in terms of what constitutes evidence and explanation, and the nature of the relationship between the two
Specifically, teachers must be prepared to conduct scientific inquiries which take into account a different set of accounts and variables, for example, affective ones concerned with the feelings of people.

A corollary to invoking and accepting girls' prior experience and knowledge is its use as avidence – and as a point of departure for both exploration and explanation. In a feminist school science, feelings, reactions, values and intuitions become important starting points for the development of principles and theories. Evidence can be unique, anecdotal, partial and partisan, and seen to be so. There is much discussion of 'soft sciences' such as sociological and psychological researches being conducted by means of 'new paradigm' methods (Reason and Rowan, 1981). What we are advocating is the use of such methods in 'hard science' and in science as it is practised in science classrooms. To us, this methodological and epistemological approach challenges the masculine heart of science, and brings to it the positive virtues of a feminist view of scientific enquiry. As such, teachers and curriculum developers must be prepared to encourage a re-examination of what constitutes evidence in scientific enquiry and make full use of, for example, interviews by pupils, drawings, narratives, case studies, diary reports and other such methods for the reporting of evidence and the conducting of enquiries.

School science must be re-written in terms of the views it has of the status of scientific knowledge
Specifically, teachers must examine carefully the philosophical and psycho-social concomitants of their learning environments. [. . .] It must be made explicit in science lessons (Manthorpe, 1982) that co-operation and valuing of the contributions of others is an overtly positive goal. A goal to be sought out and evaluated by both teachers and pupils and, more importantly, one for which the necessary skills are being overtly taught. If in masculine science we overtly teach the skills of observation, hypothesis testing and analysis, then correspondingly we must teach the skills of listening, supporting, co-operating and negotiating overtly in feminist science.

Summary

Our picture of feminist science has been developed in contrast to 'girl-friendly' and 'feminine science' and is as yet incomplete. We would argue that a school science developed towards the outline of feminist science we have generated would allow girls to grow and develop in a manner fitting their own expectations. We have drawn only some implications for the practice of science education; many more could be developed from what is said above. Throughout, our view is that it is school science, and not just girls, that must change. Nor do we dread the picture of feminist science portrayed, but revel in the fact that it 'is not afraid of the good, the speculative, the vague or the unique; indeed it openly courts them, openly confronts them and makes positive virtues of them' (Mitroff and Kilmann, 1981).

Notes

1. See Chapter 9 in this volume.

References

Bentley, D. (1984). 'Less theory more enterprise: some girls' view of science education'. Paper given at the British Psychological Conference, London.
Callaway, H. (1981). 'Women's perspectives: research as revision'. In Reason, P. and Rowan, J. (eds), *Human Inquiry: A Sourcebook of New Paradigm Research*. John Wiley & Sons.

Ebbutt, D. and Watts, D.M. (1985). 'Youngsters' perceptions of their science education, 11–16'. Secondary Science Curriculum Review.

GASAT (1985). *Proceedings of the Third International Girls and Science and Technology Conference.* University of London, Chelsea College.

Gilligan, C. (1982). *In a Different Voice: Psychological Theory and Women's Development.* Harvard University Press.

Harding, J. (1985). 'Values, cognitive style and the curriculum'. Paper presented at the Third International Girls and Science and Technology Conference, London.

Keller, E. (1983). 'Feminism as an analytic tool for the study of science'. *Academe,* Vol. 69, pp. 15–21.

Kelly, A., Whyte, J. and Smail, B. (1984) *Girls Into Science and Technology: Final Report.* University of Manchester.See Chapter 11, this volume.

MacKinnon, C.A. (1982). 'Feminism, Marxism, method and the state: an agenda for theory'. *Signs,* Vol. 7, pp. 534–35.

Manthorpe, C. (1982). 'Men's science, women's science or science: some issues related to the study of girls' science education'. *Studies in Science Education,* Vol. 9, pp. 65–80.

Manthorpe, C. (1985). 'Feminists look at science', *New Scientist,* Vol. 108, pp. 29–31.

Maxwell, N. (1984). *From Knowledge to Wisdom.* Basil Blackwell.

Mitroff, I. and Kilmann, R. (1978). *Methodological Approaches to Social Science: Integrating Divergent Concepts and Theories.* Jossey Bass.

Mitroff, I. and Kilmann, R. (1981). 'Methodological approaches to social science'. In Reason, P. and Rowan, J. (eds), *Human Inquiry: A Sourcebook of New Paradigm Research.* John Wiley & Sons.

Polanyi, M. (1964). *Science, Faith and Society.* University of Chicago Press.

Rich, A. (1972). 'When we dead awaken: writing as re-vision'. *College English,* Vol. 34, pp. 18–25.

Reason, P. and Rowan, J. (1981). *Human Inquiry: A Sourcebook of New Paradigm Research.* John Wiley & Sons.

Smail, B. (1984). *Girl-Friendly Science: Avoiding Sex Bias in the Curriculum.* Schools Council/Longman. See Chapter 9, this volume.

Part IV

Intervention Programmes

11 Girls into science and technology: final report

*Alison Kelly, Judith Whyte and
Barbara Smail*

Introduction

[. . .] Girls Into Science and Technology (GIST) was an action-research project concerned to explicate the reasons for girls' under-achievement in physical science and technical subjects at school, and simultaneously to explore the feasibility and effectiveness of interventions aimed at improving the situation. Previous research (summarized in Kelly, 1981) had documented the extent to which girls drop out of scientific subjects when these become optional and suggested some possible explanations and strategies for change. GIST hoped to explore and test some of these ideas in practice. [. . .]

GIST was designed to follow a cohort of approximately 2,000 children from the time they entered secondary school (aged 11) until they made their option choices at the end of the third year. During this time, the project team co-operated with teachers in the schools to devise and implement intervention strategies designed to alter girls' attitudes to physical science and technical craft subjects, and increase their chances of continuing these subjects into fourth and fifth year. Ten co-educational comprehensive schools in the Greater Manchester area were involved in the project, eight as 'action' and two as 'control' schools. The control schools provided data on pupils' attitudes and choices, but were not asked to attempt any interventions. The schools were not a random sample, but they served a wide variety of catchment areas from inner city to leafy suburb. [. . .]

Interventions

A large number of different interventions were attempted in schools. Much of the work of the project team was with teachers. We had less direct contact with pupils, although we did organize some events with them. However, most of the work with pupils was done by their teachers. In addition to their day to day

Source: Girls Into Science and Technology Final Report, Department of Sociology, University of Manchester, 1984.

classroom interactions, some teachers arranged special activities related to the GIST project. [. . .]

Few, if any of these interventions would have taken place if GIST had not existed. It was hoped that their effect upon the children and ultimately the school would be cumulative and qualitative. The qualitative change we aimed for was not just the sum of specific interventions but a difference in pupils' day-to-day experience of science and technology in the classroom. There was no intention to compare the effectiveness of different interventions since the same qualitative change could be achieved by many different routes.

GIST work with teachers

The interventions in schools were mainly implemented by the teachers because we felt that if there were to be any lasting changes it was imperative that these should be brought about by people who could continue the work after the project formally ended. We therefore took seriously arguments about the 'hidden curriculum' and teacher expectations. If teachers indicate by their actions – or even their tone of voice – that they are sceptical about the aims of the project or about girls' abilities in science and technology, the pupils will probably pick this up. In this way even the best-designed interventions could be rendered worthless. Conversely teachers who make only small and apparently insignificant changes in their behaviour but whose attitudes have altered as they have thought about the problems may convey positive messages to their girl pupils. For these reasons we felt that it was important for the project team to spend time with teachers, encouraging them to reflect upon their own attitudes and behaviour. [. . .]

Workshops were the first step in the process of making teachers aware of the part their own attitudes and expectations could play in perpetuating sex stereotyping in pupils' subject choice. The workshops had two main elements. We provided a good deal of information about sex differences in the classroom and research into the origins of these differences. This was intended to convince teachers that it was a serious educational problem and not one that could be wholly blamed on parents, primary schools, employers or 'society'. We also used a number of games and exercises designed to make teachers conscious of their own sex stereotypes and the way social roles and expectations operate in their classrooms (see Whyte, 1983 for further details). [. . .]

Teachers in the project schools were encouraged to develop their own ideas for interventions to try with their pupils, and to criticize and amend our ideas. However, in the initial phase it was inevitable that our ideas would be more fully worked out than the teachers', and that they would need to be convinced of our competence before trying anything too innovative. In the first year the two main strategies employed in the schools were attitude testing and the VISTA programme, both of which were mainly organized and run by the project team.

Attitude testing

An extensive programme of attitude and achievement testing was carried out with the GIST cohort in their first term at secondary school. This was both a conventional research study and an intervention in its own right. The research results have been published elsewhere (e.g. Smail and Kelly, 1984; Kelly and Smail, 1986). When the data had been analysed we produced a booklet for teachers describing what we had found and suggesting actions which might be taken on the basis of these results. We then visited each school with copies of the booklet and detailed statistics for that school, and talked to members of the science and craft departments about their pupils. This statistical yet personal approach seemed to make the information more convincing and relevant than the evidence previously presented in general terms. For example, we had argued in the initial workshops that boys would have more experience than girls of tinkering activities at home and suggested that schools might provide compensatory experiences for girls. This suggestion had little apparent impact; but when it was repeated in the context of results showing that, for example, 55 per cent of boys but only 22 per cent of girls had 'quite often' used a screwdriver, the teachers seemed to appreciate the need for compensatory experience. Several lunch-time 'clubs' for girls were subsequently started. Much of our curriculum development (Smail, 1984) was based on the survey results. For example, we suggested that physical science topics could be approached via their links with human biology, so capitalizing on both the pupils' initial interest in this area and the common surplus of lower school biology teachers. [. . .]

Classroom observations

One widely quoted classroom observation study (Spender, 1978) claims that teachers almost inevitably favour boys in class. In the workshop discussions this finding appeared to be one of the most interesting and controversial aspects of research on sex differences. Some of the teachers were already aware of the research and took a fatalistic attitude to it, others disputed it hotly. Our own classroom observation was undertaken to provide staff with some information on the way they and their pupils behaved in class. We hoped that this would clarify for teachers the mechanisms by which boys come to dominate in the laboratory and workshop, and assist them in developing techniques of classroom management to minimize male dominance.

The teachers knew that we were interested in their interactions with girls and boys, so their behaviour in this respect was certainly different from normal because of our presence. However, we felt that this was beneficial in that they were practising an egalitarian distribution of their time. If practised frequently enough this should become second nature. At the end of each period of observation we discussed our findings, both quantitative and qualitative, with the teacher so that s/he got immediate feedback on the experience of being observed. [. . .]

Options and careers

As the GIST cohort entered their third year at secondary school the project began to concentrate more on the option choices for fourth and fifth year that the children would soon be making. In many cases pupils make these choices with little real thought about their consequences for future career prospects. Conventions and stereotypes abound. We wanted to link the option choices to careers education in a broad sense (i.e. not advice about particular careers but information about a variety of life-styles and opportunities).

The previous year's option booklets were collected from all action schools and detailed comments made on their content. Comments covered topics such as timetabling, which made it difficult to take a mixture of traditional 'girls' and traditional 'boys' subjects together, and language, which implied that only one sex took a subject. In fact both these faults were encouragingly rare. We proposed alterations where the description of a subject seemed rather technical and offputting and suggested that links be made between subjects and careers which appealed to both sexes. Many of these alterations have been incorporated into the revised options booklets.

More general comments on options and careers were incorporated in a booklet (Whyte *et al.*, 1982) which was distributed to the schools. This contained suggestions on how to help the pupils to think seriously about their option choices, and information on women's changing world of work. It also contained appendix lists of resources for careers and life-style education; jobs that require or use scientific or technical qualifications; and non-traditional jobs that might appeal to 'feminine' interests.

Wider contacts

As well as working directly with the eight project schools, we have spent some time on a wider range of contacts. The project has attracted considerable publicity, including features in two television programmes, several radio broadcasts and numerous newspaper and magazine articles. We have had over 1,000 enquiries from individuals, mainly teachers, and our publications and bibliography have been widely distributed. The project team has received more requests to speak than we could possibly handle and although we were forced to turn down many invitations, we did consider publicity to be an important part of our work. Girls' underachievement in science and technology is closely linked to society's attitude towards women. Publicizing the problem and our work has undoubtedly contributed to changing attitudes and this in turn may feed back to schools. Moreover media interest can give a boost to teachers' morale within the project schools. [. . .]

The VISTA programme

One of the major intervention strategies throughout the GIST project was the VISTA programme, a series of visits to schools by women working in science and technology. The aim of the visits was to provide the children with role models of women working in 'masculine' occupations who enjoyed their work and were successful at it. Ideally they should have an attractive and vivacious personality and be leading active personal and family lives. In this way we hoped to counter the image of the woman scientist as an oddity and reassure the girls that studying science did not mean abandoning all their existing dreams of adult life. We also wanted to de-stereotype the remote impersonal image of science and technology by stressing the links between the work the VISTA visitors were doing and what the children were learning in class (Smail, 1982).

Women were recruited for this programme through letters to the press and contact with local employers. Volunteers were coached in ways of talking to 11 to 13 year olds by the GIST team. They often needed some help in picking out bits of their jobs which would appeal to this age group and in simplifying their language to match the children's vocabulary.

Whenever possible visits to schools were arranged so that the woman's work was linked to the topic the children were currently studying. For example, when they were learning about acids and alkalis there was a food technologist who brought cakes made from cake mixes with incorrectly balanced baking powder to show the use of pH measurements in the food industry. At first most of the VISTA visitors were graduates, but as the project progressed John Catton made particular efforts to recruit younger and less highly qualified women (e.g. trainee plumbers and motor mechanics). Children often found it easier to identify with these women, but unfortunately they were less likely than the graduates to have the verbal skills and self-confidence to face a school class on their own. So we tried to arrange that they visited schools in groups and spent more time on practical demonstrations.

VISTA was evaluated by requesting teachers to fill in a report form after each visit; pupils were asked at the end of the project which visits they remembered, how they rated them, and what were the best and worst aspects of these visits. Most teachers thought the VISTA visits were a success. A few of the women used language that was too difficult for the children, but the majority of them avoided this trap and provided an interesting talk. Many teachers commented that the boys were more involved in question and answer sessions than the girls; they also remarked that the pupils did not seem to appreciate that the visitors were women doing traditionally male jobs.

The children's evaluation of the visits was also generally favourable, with the girls being somewhat more enthusiastic than the boys. Girls in particular said that they appreciated the opportunity to learn about a range of different jobs and to see women in these jobs. This indicates that the role modelling aspects of the visits *was* noticed by the children. Both girls and boys said they enjoyed demonstrations and asking questions, but were not so keen on visits where they had to sit and listen; this distinction was echoed in the teachers' comments. [. . .]

Roadshows: 'Whatever you choose to do, it's OK'
Despite the information in the *Options and Careers* booklet, many teachers were reluctant to embark on activities designed to question traditional values and life-styles. However they were usually willing for the project team to undertake such sessions with their classes. As option choice approached we organized a

'Whatever you choose to do, it's OK' day in each school. Typically there might be a film such as 'Jobs for the Girls', about a girl who wants to be a motor mechanic, with a follow-up discussion; then perhaps a tour of the careers exhibition and finding the answers to a quiz which were all hidden in the display materials. Then the class would meet a group of three or four visitors who had non-traditional jobs. For this we recruited not only women engineers, car mechanics, carpenters, etc., but also male nurses, cookery teachers, men who look after young children and a house-husband with career wife. Finally the pupils were encouraged to explore their own strengths and weaknesses, likes and dislikes in a game organized by their form tutor, so that they could better identify the jobs to which they would be suited.

Many boys, and to a lesser extent girls, revealed very traditional and rigid attitudes about the separate roles of women and men in society. Despite their first-hand knowledge of working mothers and one-parent families we found children often had a stereotyped view of their future life, with the woman as full time homemaker and the husband as full time breadwinner. Nevertheless they appeared to enjoy discussion of alternative views and possibilities. Many children came up at the end of the day to tell us of the non-traditional choices they would like to make. However, some boys were uncomfortable with alternative views; as a group they exhibited some hostility to the male visitors, and frequently queried their sexuality (Catton and Smail, 1983). Although not specifically asked to comment on the male visitors in their evaluations of VISTA, many pupils did so (perhaps because they were fresh in their minds). It was noticeable that the boys rated the men significantly worse than the girls did, and worse than they rated the women visitors. [. . .]

Outcomes

Option choices
One of the main aims of the project was to encourage more girls to choose physical science and technical craft subjects when these became optional in fourth and fifth year. However, option choices fluctuate from year to year, and one year's choice cannot be interpreted in isolation. Figure 1 shows the percentage of the year group of girls and boys taking physics at each school, in the GIST cohort and in each of the three preceding years.

The message from these option choices is ambiguous. Figure 1 shows that a higher proportion of girls chose physics in the GIST cohort than in any of the previous three years at four of the action schools (Ashgrove, Edgehill, Moss Green and Tall Trees). The increases ranged from 13 to 5 per cent. However, the two control schools also had a higher proportion of girls taking physics in the GIST cohort than in the previous years! At three other action schools there was little change, while at one (Hamlet) there was a clear drop in the percentage of girls choosing physics. Among boys there was much less variation. Only at Hamlet (where there was again a drop) and the control school Burnbank (with a striking increase) did the GIST cohort deviate from the pattern of previous years. [. . .]

There are three main points to bear in mind when interpreting these option choices. First, it is important to remember that in the normal course of events option choices fluctuate from year to year, sometimes quite widely, so it is difficult to know how much of the variation in the action year can be attributed to GIST interventions. Secondly, it is possible that the control schools were affected by their participation in the project so that the action/control distinction was blurred. Third, as the Figure shows, there are marked differences between schools which persist from year to year.

Fluctuations in the uptake of a particular subject from year to year can have many causes. Sometimes they can be traced directly to the influence of one teacher or to policy changes within the school. In other instances the effect may be due to variations in the ability of the year group, to groups of friends deciding to do something together, or to an unusual event such as a film or visitor.

The issue of random fluctuation from year to year was explored with the heads of science and heads of physics of the two control schools, who were asked why they thought more girls (and boys in the case of Burnbank) were taking physics in the GIST cohort. Teachers at both schools initially declared themselves mystified and felt that it was a statistical fluke. On reflection the staff at New Hall suggested that changes in the option system might have had some influence. Physics was in a column with largely practical subjects for the GIST cohort, and at this middle class school most parents preferred their children to take academic subjects; in previous years it had been in a column with the second languages which probably siphoned off many able girls. However, at Burnbank there was a straight choice between physics and commerce and this had not changed. [. . .]

GIST did not conform to a classical experimental model in that both staff and pupils in the control schools knew they were involved in an experiment, and the staff knew of its purpose. Teachers at both control schools felt that the act of filling in the questionnaires might have made the children think a bit, and the teachers themselves were almost certainly affected by their involvement with the project. However, they denied that they had made any greater efforts than usual to encourage girls to take physics. They also denied that their own or their colleagues' behaviour had been in the least influenced by their participation in GIST. This reaction was also common among teachers in the action schools and should perhaps not be taken at face value.

Figure 1 shows that there is considerable variation between schools in the percentage of girls and boys taking physics. For example, over 25 per cent of all girls at Edgehill regularly took physics in fourth year, compared to under 10 per cent at Green Park. Much of this variation can be attributed to social class. The two unambiguously middle class schools in the sample (Edgehill and New Hall) both had a high proportion of girls (and boys) studying physics. On the other hand the schools with very small proportions of girls taking physics (Green Park, Moss Green and Burnbank) were all located in working class areas.

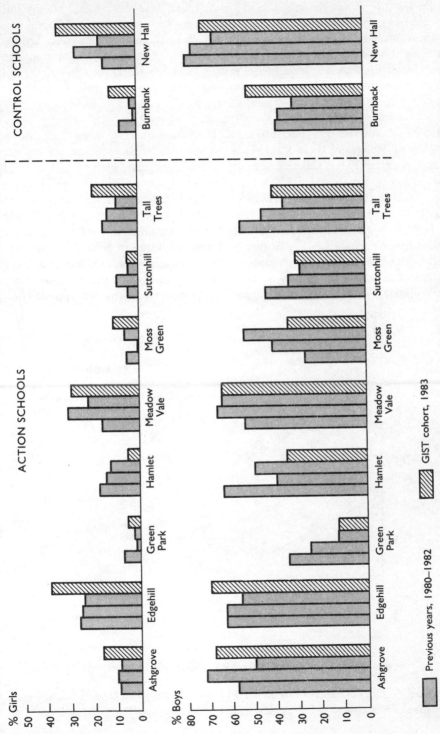

Figure 1. The percentage of girls and boys in the year group at GIST schools taking physics in fourth year, 1980–3.

However, this is not the whole story. Individual teachers, option systems and school ethos also have some effect. Edgehill has a less affluent school population than New Hall, but a higher proportion of girls choosing physics, largely because of a faculty structure which requires most pupils to take either physics or chemistry. Meadow Vale has a mixed catchment area but a strong and effective science department with a tradition of encouraging girls. [. . .]

Pupil's attitude changes
Children's attitudes are probably a more sensitive measure than their option choices of changes in their opinions about science, technology and sex typing. They are certainly less influenced by structural constraints such as the nature of the option system or the size of a teaching group. Changes in children's scores show many significant differences between pupils' attitude changes in the action and control schools. [. . .] The changes in sex stereotyping are shown in Figure 2. Both girls and boys in action schools came to see much less difference in the suitability of various jobs for women and men. Children in control schools also became less stereotyped (presumably this is a maturation effect) but to a lesser extent than those in action schools. In addition children became more enthusiastic about taking up jobs traditionally associated with the opposite sex,

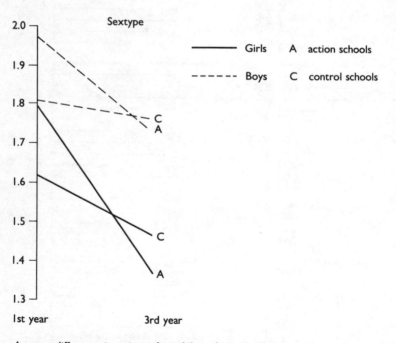

Average difference in ratings of suitability of jobs for women and men

Figure 2. The mean scores of girls and boys in action and control schools on a measure of sex stereotyping in first and third year.

and this was most marked among girls in action schools. These action/control differences are consistent with a causal effect of the children's exposure to the roadshow visits by women and men working in non-traditional jobs. [. . .]

As far as general attitudes to science are concerned, the action/control differences were smaller, but still significant. The data for Image of Science and Science Curiosity has been analysed in some detail (Kelly, 1986) and they show a small but consistent trend for children in action schools to have less negative attitude changes than children in control schools. This was true for LIKESCI (personal liking for science), SCIWORLD (impact of science on society) and PHYSCUR (desire to learn about physical science). These scales are related to GIST interventions such as monitoring classroom interactions and promoting curriculum development, which attempted to affect the pupils' daily experience of science. It is noticeable that, contrary to the fears of some teachers, boys' attitudes were at least as positively affected as girls'. The implication is that what is good for girls in science is also good for boys.

There were also some differences between children in action and control schools on other questionnaires. Girls in action schools were more likely to mention a job with some scientific or technical content as their expected or desired occupation. This is one of the most pleasing results, as it shows that the GIST project has opened up new opportunities to girls of a kind they would not have considered before. Children in action schools were significantly more likely than children in control schools to say that there were no school subjects at which one sex was better than the other. Action school girls were also more likely to want to be employed while they had young children, and less likely to say they wanted their future husband to be cleverer than themselves. On the other hand boys in the action schools were less willing to take a share in the housework if their wives were at home with children.

Attitudes did not vary as much as option choices between schools. However, pupils at Edgehill had consistently better attitudes in third year than would have been predicted on the basis of their first year scores. Pupils at Ashgrove and Suttonhill had consistently poor attitude changes, as did the two control schools, Burnbank and New Hall. The reasons for this variation are discussed in the GIST book (Whyte, 1986). [. . .]

Teacher's attitudes
Most of the GIST interventions were implemented by teachers working with their own classes, and their attitudes were crucial in determining the success of these strategies. Teachers' attitudes were studied in a variety of ways. After each visit to a school we made notes on what had happened, which included comments on the teachers' responses. These notes provide a record of the way in which the commitment of individuals and departments varied during the course of the project. [. . .] They reveal considerable alterations in teachers' attitudes, although these were by no means uniform. Perhaps a typical reaction from a male science teacher was for an initial scepticism to change gradually into endorsement and even enthusiasm over the first couple of years of the project's

work in schools, as it became evident that GIST had practical ideas and could implement them efficiently (e.g. by organizing the VISTA programme and attitude testing, and producing useable curriculum materials). Although there were many exceptions we found that in general, craft staff were more resistant to the aims of the project than science staff. [. . .] The sex of the teacher seemed to make little difference. Some women science teachers sympathized with the girls' problems, but others seemed to think that since they had succeeded in science there was no real problem. [. . .]

We also invited an independent team of evaluators – three male sociologists – to talk to the teachers about their impressions of the project, and to assess the way their opinions and classroom practices had altered. [. . .] They were invited into four action schools: in one we judged the project to have been successful, two fair and one unsuccessful. [. . .] We did not arrange this until the final year of the project, so the evaluators had to rely on teachers' own accounts of their changing attitudes, rather than observing changes over time. [. . .]

With one exception all the teachers interviewed were well aware of the existence of the project and could talk for long periods about its aims and methods. The aims were generally perceived as being to do with encouraging girls in science and technical crafts and making these subjects more attractive to girls. Only four teachers (out of 34 interviewed) gave changing teachers' attitudes or behaviour as an aim, and only one mentioned changing women's position in society. As Payne *et al.* (1984) comment: 'the project was largely viewed as interventionist in the lives of pupils rather than the lives of teachers'. Perhaps for this reason teachers were seldom able to point to changes in their own behaviour. To quote the report again: 'on balance staff seem almost grudging to concede that there have been even marginal changes in their classroom practice'. As the authors point out this may well be a defensive reaction: 'to admit to changes (perhaps to be aware of changes) in one's own practices . . . might be tantamount to accepting that there were inadequacies . . . there being inequality of treatment for half their clients'. Nevertheless many teachers described aspects of their classroom practice which can be traced directly to GIST:

> she always takes opportunities in her lessons to question sex stereotyping . . . (p. 27)

> he has thought more about the use of extended writing (p. 20)

> textbooks are now more closely scrutinized in terms of what activities of boys and girls are contained in them (p. 33)

> Certainly the project has altered her teaching. She is more conscious of making efforts to involve girls. Her stress is on classroom management, teaching style, questioning strategies – she mentions trying to find more appropriate curriculum materials. (p. 19)

These comments are consistent with the evidence from our field notes. The evaluators' report concludes that 'some teachers *did* point to changes for themselves, that some *did* point to changes in their colleagues and that there *were* organizational changes. . . . Given the general reluctance to refer to changes . . . these perceived changes stand out as important successes for the GIST project' (italics in original).

Overall the impression from this evaluation is of teachers who were neutral or mildly supportive towards the project, with a few cases of hostility. The hostility mainly emanated from the school where we had judged the project unsuccessful. This school was the only one in the action group to segregate the sexes for crafts at the beginning of the project. Despite the teachers' expressed feelings, they had not only ceased to do this by the end of the project but had joined with another action school in a 'positive discrimination' initiative to give girls non-traditional work experience. The clash of values between the highly sex segregated atmosphere of this school and the GIST aims seemed to have been acutely felt by the teachers, of whom much greater changes of belief, attitude and practice were demanded than in any other school. [. . .]

Changing the climate

The most important effects of GIST may be virtually unmeasurable. They have certainly not been measured, as they were unanticipated. They can be described as a 'ripple' effect which the project has produced, not just in the GIST schools, or locally in Manchester, but in schools and teachers throughout the country, and even amongst an interested international audience.

The issue of girls' underachievement in science and technology is much more widely debated now than it was when GIST began. It is the subject of numerous reports, articles and discussion. Educationalists from the Secretary of State to classroom teachers have argued that encouraging girls in science should have high priority. The year 1984 has been declared Women in Science and Engineering (WISE) year, and events, some of which originated with GIST, are being held throughout the country. Although we would certainly not want to claim all the credit we do feel that GIST has contributed to this changing climate. Publicity about the project appears to have reached not only science teachers but policy makers and educators generally. It has made teachers (and others) aware of the problem and shown that it is not insuperable. Our bibliography and booklets have been widely distributed and quoted, and appear to have constituted an intervention in schools other than the eight directly involved in the project. Press reports and television and radio programmes have contributed to the process of making girls and science a serious educational issue. [. . .]

Assessment

GIST has been successful in that it has refined our understanding of girls' and boys' attitudes and stereotypes about science, and the process of option choices. The specific focus of interventions was the stereotyping of science and technology as masculine, and in this respect the children's attitudes were considerably modified. Children's option choices (a behavioural phenomenon) are strongly affected by their daily experiences of school subjects, and this was less susceptible to GIST interventions. Some teachers' attitudes, no less than their behaviour, altered in the desired direction. Finally, there is evidence that changes in group behaviour were more likely to occur in schools and departments where the prevailing ethos comfortably incorporated GIST concerns. [. . .]

Acknowledgement

The Girls Into Science and Technology Project was funded by the Joint Panel of the Equal Opportunities Commission and the Social Science Research Council, the Schools Council, the Department of Industry Education Unit and Shell U.K. Ltd. John Catton worked on the project as Schools Liaison Officer for Craft Design Technology; Vera Ferguson and Dolores Donegan provided secretarial assistance. We are grateful to all our sponsors and co-workers, although they do not necessarily share the views expressed here.

References

Catton, J. and Smail, B. (1983). 'Removing the blinkers', *Women and Education Newsletter*, No. 25.

Kelly, A. (ed.) (1981). *The Missing Half: Girls and Science Education*. Manchester University Press.

Kelly, A. (1986). 'The development of children's attitudes to science: a longitudinal study', *European Journal of Science Education*, Vol. 8, pp. 399–412.

Kelly, A. and Smail, B. (1986). 'Sex stereotypes and attitudes to science among eleven-year-old children'. *British Journal of Educational Psychology*, Vol. 56, pp. 158–68.

Payne, G., Hustler, D. and Cuff, T. (1984). *GIST or PIST: Teachers' Perceptions of the Project 'Girls Into Science and Technology'*. Manchester Polytechnic.

Smail, B. (1982). 'Changing the image of women scientists', *Women and Training News*, No. 9, p. 11, Winter.

Smail, B. (1984). *Girl-Friendly Science: Avoiding Sex-Bias in the Curriculum*. Schools Council/Longman. See Chapter 9, this volume.

Smail, B. and Kelly, A. (1984). 'Sex differences in science and technology among 11 year old school children: I Cognitive; II Affective', *Research in Science and Technological Education*, Vol. 2, pp. 61–76; 87–106.

Spender, D. (1978). 'Don't talk, listen', *Times Educational Supplement*, 3rd November.

Whyte, J. (1983). 'Courses for teachers on sex differences and sex typing', *Journal of Education for Teaching*, October.

Whyte, J. (1986). *Girls Into Science and Technology: the Story of a Project*. Routledge & Kegan Paul.

Whyte, J., Kelly, A., Smail, B. and Catton, J. (1982). *GIST: Options and Careers*. Manchester Polytechnic.

12   Encouraging girls to give physics a second chance

Barbara Smail

In Britain, able pupils face option choices twice in their school careers. First at 14+ they must choose seven or eight subjects to study for O level or CSE examinations. Those continuing beyond 16+ must choose again. Pupils in Scotland choose four to six subjects for 'Higher' examinations which are taken at 17. In England, Wales and Northern Ireland, pupils select only two or three subjects for A level examinations at 18. Table 1 shows the percentage of girls and boys gaining O level passes in physics who choose physics a second time for Higher or A level. For comparison, the figures for English literature are included in the table. Two interesting trends can be seen in these figures:

(i)   In Scotland, where pupils choose more subjects, a higher proportion of girls continue with physics than in the rest of Britain.

(ii)   The figures for girls in England, Wales and Northern Ireland show that the percentage who choose physics a second time is not dissimilar to the percentage who choose English literature for A level. There are sex differences in subject choice with twice as many boys taking physics as taking English, while four times as many girls take English as take Physics. In Scotland, the numbers of boys and girls taking English for 'Higher' is more comparable because English and maths are compulsory at this level in most schools.

This paper discusses some of the results of an evaluation carried out in 1983 and 1984 of three-day residential courses aimed at girls who had gained an O level or O grade pass in physics. The courses were designed to encourage the girls to opt for physics a second time and to consider the possibility of physics-based degree courses.

The courses and the evaluation were funded by the Equal Opportunities Commission. Three university physics departments were involved, at Glasgow, Manchester and Sussex.

Source: Paper presented to Third International Girls and Science and Technology Conference, England, 1985. First published in this volume. © Open University Press 1987.

Table 1. Percentage of eligible girls and boys making a second choice for physics

	England, Wales and N. Ireland		Scotland	
	Girls	*Boys*	*Girls*	*Boys*
Physics				
Number gaining A–C in O level (1980) / Number gaining O grade (1982)	26,016	76,156	5,461	12,466
Number entering A level (1982) / Number entering Higher (1983)	11,259	44,469	3,578	10,325
% of those eligible taking A level / taking Higher	43.4	58.5	65.5	82.8
English				
Number gaining A–C in O level (1980) / Number gaining O grade (1982)	95,209	56,271	24,853	18,176
Number entering A level (1982) / Number entering Higher (1983)	44,386	19,003	20,024	16,084
% of those eligible taking A level / taking Higher	46.6	33.8	80.5	88.5

The design and purpose of the evaluation

It was hoped that the evaluation would provide answers to the following questions:

(i)   are the courses effective in increasing the number of girls continuing with physics?
(ii) which parts of the course are most effective in promoting physics choice?
(iii) how might the courses develop to increase their effectiveness?
(iv) are there other unanticipated beneficial outcomes of such courses?

The evaluation employed a variety of research techniques, including postal questionnaires, tape-recorded individual semi-structured interviews and participant observation.

The courses

At all three centres, the courses have been very popular with local schools. In both years, the number of applicants far exceeded the number of available places. To avoid discouraging those girls who were not offered places on the three-day residential courses, one-day short courses were organized. These one-day events also proved popular and successful.

Each of the three-day courses catered for about 60 girls and contained six lectures on a variety of topics selected by the organizing committees, several tutorials, two or three afternoons of practical work, a careers panel discussion, a visit to a scientific place of interest (e.g. an observatory or power station) and social events such as discos and theatre visits. A successful pilot course had been organized in 1982 by the Manchester Physics Department and this was used as the basic model for the courses in 1983 when Glasgow and Sussex became involved. At the original Manchester course lectures, concentrated on energy and astronomy, but later courses have included lectures on more varied topics such as 'low-temperature physics', 'physics in medical diagnosis', 'physics of sound', etc. Both Sussex courses have had the underlying theme of 'waves' and Glasgow used local experts to show the applications of physics in many fields, e.g. the oil industry, medicine, archaeology, etc.

At Manchester, three undergraduate teaching laboratories were in use each afternoon. The girls undertook a range of investigations on optics, electronics and radioactivity in groups of two or three. At Glasgow, practical work involved electronics, making an optic-fibre communication link, and radioactivity. At Sussex, the laboratory work reflected the 'waves' theme, including investigations of visible spectra and the Doppler effect.

There were variations between the three centres in the focus of the organizing committees and their perceptions of the causes of girls' avoidance of physics. The course at Sussex was introduced by a session called 'You and Your Future', organized by two women careers advisers from the university staff. The purpose of this session was to give the participants some information about career opportunities, using physics as a direct and indirect qualification, to challenge stereotypes about physics and physicists and to start the tutorial groups working together effectively. The session used small group discussion to clarify what the girls wanted from the course. They also spent part of the afternoon making a collage entitled 'A physicist'. This revealed that physicists are thought of as male, brainy, hard-working, untidy and poorly dressed. The plenary discussion demonstrated that the stereotype is inaccurate, although there might be some truth in some of its aspects. This introduction at Sussex produced an emphasis on the stereotyping of physics in the course. At Glasgow and Manchester, the organizers felt that girls opt out of physics because it is seen as boring, and the issue of the masculinity of physics was not raised overtly. They focused on trying to show that physics can be exciting.

All three centres had difficulty in finding women to help run the course. Postgraduate and third or fourth year undergraduate women acted as group tutors and laboratory demonstrators, but there were no women lecturers in any of the three departments in 1983. At Manchester, the two women post-doctoral fellows and a visiting woman lecturer from Southampton University gave lectures, balancing the three lectures given by men from the department. Glasgow and Sussex also tried to achieve a 50:50 balance by drawing on women from industry and government research establishments. In 1984, possibly as a result of the course, Glasgow had recruited its first woman faculty member, and the Manchester post-doctoral fellows were departing for posts in other universities!

The one-day courses were abbreviated versions of the three-day courses, involving two or three lectures, a tutorial and a careers panel. At Manchester, a practical session was included.

The effect of the courses

Various comparisons can be made to assess the effectiveness of the courses. Table 2 shows the results. First, the take-up of physics by course participants can be compared with the national averages from Table 1. Looked at in this way, the results are impressive, but they raise the question: is this really the effect of the course or were the group pre-selected to include mainly girls who would have taken physics with or without the course?

Comparing the take-up figures with those for a control group of girls who were nominated for the three-day course, but could not be accommodated, might be fairer. However, the comparison is partly confounded because the majority of these girls did attend a one-day course. Apart from the Sussex 1983 course, the three-day course does seem to have a positive effect, enhancing the uptake by 12 to 40 per cent.

The difficulty of eliminating effects due to selection bias is demonstrated by

Table 2. Percentage of the three-day course participants choosing physics compared with girls who chose the three-day course but actually attended a one-day course, and the national figures.

Centre	1983		1984		National Figures 1982
	3-day	1-day	3-day	1-day	
Glasgow	93	81	89	77	65.5
Manchester	80	64	64	54	
Sussex	65	78	78	38	43.4

the drop in Manchester figures from 1983 to 1984. In 1983, the letter to teachers asking for candidates for the course stated clearly that the course was intended for girls who were *doubtful* about choosing physics for A level. However, it was obvious from girls' comments during and after the course that many teachers were sending girls who had already definitely chosen physics. In 1984, the Manchester organizing committee re-emphasized that the course was for the uncommitted and also asked for the pupils' grades and class position in physics and a foreign language and/or English. The course participants were selected to include girls performing equally well in arts and sciences. In previous years, more girls from private, grammar and girls-only schools had been selected for the course at Manchester. In 1984, a majority of the course participants came from mixed state comprehensive schools. Thus, the Manchester figures for 1984 probably provide a reasonably valid assessment of the course effect, increasing the uptake by about 20 per cent over national figures, but only 10 per cent over a comparable group attending a one-day course.

From the girls' reports immediately following the course and letters received up to 12 months after attending a course, it seems that the aspects which are most important in changing girls' attitudes to physics are:

(i)   the practical sessions;
(ii) the real-life applications of physics;
(iii) the extension of physics into areas areas not covered in the school physics course and in which the department has active research interests;
(iv) the residential nature of the course, the opportunity to meet girls with similar interests and to see what life at university is like.

Negative comments concern the standard of the lectures, which often matched undergraduate understanding better than that of O level candidates, and some of the attempts to give careers advice. At Sussex, the tutorials led by graduate and undergraduate students were praised for their usefulness, but, at the other centres, the tutorials were not always successful. The topics which most engaged the girls' interests were astronomy, radioactivity applications in medicine, archaeology, fibre optics, electronics, thermography, liquid crystals, colour and quarks.

Conclusion

From the evidence available, the effect of the course on the girls who took part seems to be generally very positive. I interviewed some of the girls who came on the course but chose not to do physics in the spring term of their first year in the sixth form. Of these, one girl had chosen French, German and economics initially, but changed from German to physics after one term. She explained her initial choice by saying that, although she had enjoyed the course, she had been persuaded by her sixth form adviser that German 'fitted' better with French and economics than physics. Her physics teacher reported that now she had changed subjects, she was working with such motivation and determination that he expected her to catch up and do well. He could only attribute this enthusiasm to the 'Women and Physics' course. This girl's case illustrates the difficulty many pupils have in choosing only three A level subjects. The Scottish system, which allows for pupils to maintain a wider range of subjects, both arts and sciences, seems to enable more girls to choose physics. Current proposals before the DES for a broadening of the sixth-form curriculum in England, Wales and Northern Ireland may eventually alleviate the problem.

The effect of running a 'Women and Physics' course on the organizers and their departments also seems to have been beneficial. Certainly, all three departments are now keen to recruit women staff as soon as suitable candidates present themselves. They are also rather disappointed that the course has not dramatically increased the number of girls applying to them for degree courses this year. But it may take several years of courses for such an effect to show up. Of the first group of girls to attend a course (Manchester, 1982), 6 (10 per cent) are now first year undergraduates for physics degrees at other universities, while 10 (17 per cent) are training for medical careers, including pharmacy, opthalmic optics, medical technicians and nursing, and 12 (20 per cent) are taking other scientific degrees. Similar figures were obtained from a follow-up study of girls attending the Glasgow 1983 course, who after their one-year Higher course, are now at university or in employment. It seems that girls who do physics see their future in applied fields, particularly medicine and the biological sciences, rather than as pure physicists. For physics departments worried about the quality and gender of their intake, courses at 16+ are the start of a solution. The courses have caused those concerned to look more closely at their own attitudes and values. But much still needs to be done in schools and through the media to portray physics in a way which does not alienate those creative young people that the subject and the society so desperately need.

13 Increasing the participation and achievement of girls and women in mathematics, science and engineering

Elizabeth K. Stage, Nancy Kreinberg, Jacquelynne Eccles (Parsons) and Joanne Rossi Becker

Women have made substantial inroads in the last 15 years into the fields of mathematics, science and engineering in the United States. The proportion of women earning doctorates in science and engineering, for example, has risen from 7 per cent in 1965 to 25 per cent in 1980 (National Research Council, 1980). As Figure 1 shows, however, most of this increase is attributable to large proportions of women in the social and life sciences; women are still at or below 12 per cent of the PhDs in mathematics, the physical sciences and engineering. At the undergraduate level, the proportion of women planning majors in science and engineering also has been increasing (Cooperative Institutional Research Program, 1974–82). The greatest percentage increase has been in the field of engineering, in which there were 358 women who earned bachelor's degrees in 1970, representing 0.8 per cent of the graduating class, and 5,680 women in 1980 representing 9.7 per cent of the graduating class. With a projection for 1984 of 14 per cent, it is clear that there have been impressive inroads in the area of engineering. Yet, at this rate of 1 per cent per year, it will be 2020 before there are equal numbers of women and men earning engineering degrees! [. . .]

It is our contention that the close relationship between research and development activities related to women's participation in math-related fields is an important catalyst for advancement in both research and development. A good example is the research of the Berkeley sociologist, Lucy Sells, who investigated the persistence of women and minorities in different doctoral fields (Sells, 1975). She found that mathematics training in secondary schools was a

Source: Klein, S.S. (ed.), *Achieving Sex Equity through Education*, A. Johns Hopkins University Press, 1985.

'critical filter' for these groups, keeping many students from studying various scientific fields as undergraduate or graduate students. Her personal enthusiasm prompted the founding of the Math/Science Network, now a group of 1,000 scientists, educators and community people who work together to promote the participation of women in math-related and non-traditional fields. The popularization of the 'critical filter' idea (Ernest, 1976) caused many educators to take an interest in secondary school mathematics course enrollments. [. . .]

Two years ago, the American Association for the Advancement of Science (AAAS) prepared an inventory of programs for women and girls in mathematics, science and engineering (Aldrich and Hall, 1980). It covered projects started in the United States since 1966 and ended data collection in 1978. While such an inventory can never be complete, it included 315 projects. Observing that only half of the directors of NSF-funded career days for college women had completed the requested summaries, one of the authors has estimated that there may easily have been twice as many programs in all of the categories (Aldrich,

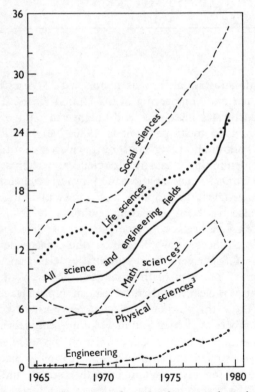

Figure 1.   Women as a percentage of total science and engineering doctorate recipients by field: 1965–80.

Source: Vetter, 1981.
[1] Includes psychology.
[2] Includes computer sciences.
[3] Includes environmental sciences (earth sciences, oceanography, and atmospheric sciences).

1982). Realizing that it is impossible to do justice to as many as 600 programs, we will first summarize the characteristics of programs in the directory, then turn to descriptions of model programs.

Of the 315 projects in the AAAS directory, more than a third covered six or more fields of science, nearly all of which included mathematics. Of those projects that covered five or fewer fields, engineering (the focus of half) was the most popular. Approximately one fifth of the programs concentrated exclusively on mathematics. The projects were distributed throughout the educational system in almost a normal curve with respect to age – that is, a few at elementary, more in junior high and high schools, and the largest number at the undergraduate level, with a tapering off at the graduate and faculty development levels. The projects were also distributed widely around the country, and nearly all of them (84 per cent) were university-based. [. . .]

Special classes for women

Several projects have experimented with all-female environments, indicating that there may be some advantage to female students from spending some of the instructional time in single-sex settings. All of the projects described below, however, used several strategies in conjunction with the exclusion of males, so that they cannot be said to test a single-sex setting *per se*.

Maths for girls

In 1973, the Lawrence Hall of Science, which offers after-school classes in mathematics, computer science and the sciences, found that fewer than 25 per cent of the participants were girls. To attract girls to the Hall and to inform them and their parents that mathematics is an appropriate topic for girls to study, a 'Math for Girls' course was established. The course, which aims to increase positive attitudes towards mathematics and to increase problem-solving skills, has four problem-solving strands: (1) logic, strategies, and patterns; (2) breaking set; (3) creative thinking, estimating, and observing; and (4) spatial visualization. The eight 1½ to 2 hour sessions are taught by a young woman who uses mathematics in her studies (often a University of California science major) or in her career, who establishes a co-operative, recreational atmosphere.

The course has not had the resources to conduct a formal evaluation. The original goal, to increase young women's participation in Hall course offerings, has been met in part, as female enrollment in other courses has increased from 25 to 40 per cent. The role of the 'Math for Girls' course in influencing this progress cannot be disentangled from several other Lawrence Hall of Science outreach efforts, however. The course does remain popular, though, and a handbook that gives a detailed curriculum guide for the course has sold 2,500 copies (Downie *et al*, 1981).

An acceleration program for mathematically gifted girls
The Johns Hopkins University Study of Mathematically Precocious Youth
(SMPY) was established in 1971 to identify mathematically precocious youth
and to encourage their talent by tailoring educational experiences to their needs.
[. . .] The program was far more successful in identifying and accelerating the
progress of boys than of girls (Fox, 1976), so that an experimental program was
started just for girls.

The program and its evaluation are described in Fox (1976) and Brody and
Fox (1980). Designed to counter the formal, competitive, and theoretical
conditions which observation and interviews indicated as factors diminishing
the girls' success in the co-educational class, the girls' class was taught in an
informal, co-operative style by three women. The relevance of mathematics
to social problems was stressed through rewritten mathematics problems and
speakers who described interesting fields, such as operations research, in which
mathematics is used to solve social problems. Female role models also discussed
their combination of interesting mathematics-related careers with raising
families.
class than the co-educational class had been, and the completion rate was similar
to the females' rate in the co-educational classes. Eighteen of the 27 girls
completed the experimental class, meaning that they had learned Algebra I over
a three-month summer period, meeting about four hours a week. Their
performance on a ninth grade normed Algebra I test was at the 89th percentile,
significantly higher than that of control boys and girls who had been matched
from the SMPY sample for SAT scores. [. . .]

An experiment at the college level
A special section of a mathematics course for women has also been tried
successfully at the college level. In 1974–5, the University of Missouri-Kansas
City conducted an NSF-funded project that offered a special section of the
introductory mathematics sequence (MacDonald, 1980). This section enrolled
33 students in the first semester and 22 in the second semester, compared with
55 to 60 students in the regular sections. Taught by a female professor and a
female advanced graduate student, the class was preceded by a one-hour
optional tutoring session in which students worked in small groups in a social,
informal atmosphere. Other supplemental activities included discussions of the
socialization of women, services available to students on campus, social and
cultural issues, and personal experiences. Students were given take-home
review tests and had the chance to take each test a second time, counting the
second score if better, or the average if not. A comparison of participants in the
special course with women in the regular sections showed that they had higher
grades and a better completion rate. While the retaking of tests may have
contributed to higher grades, the women in the special section had been selected
because of weaker backgrounds. Women in the special section also reported
greater satisfaction with the course than those in the regular sections, and they
reported that they had spent more time studying mathematics. It is not possible

to determine which of the many differences contributed to success, but 56 per cent of the participants went on to enroll in another mathematics course, compared with 17 per cent of the women in other sections.

Retention of women in the science disciplines
A program at Purdue University combined intensive counseling – a course that offered students the opportunity to meet women scientists – and spcial laboratory projects for freshman students in an effort to increase the retention of women in undergraduate science majors; it was found that the effects of these interventions were cumulative (Brown, 1976). In the special projects, students were assigned to small laboratory groups to work on projects directly with professors, an experience not usually given to freshmen. Although no female reported experiencing discrimination in the laboratory situation, it was found that the greatest percentage of female students who completed the project and reported the greatest personal satisfaction were participants in either all-female groups or groups in which females were at least half of the group membership. The sex composition of the group did not have a similar effect on the male students. The author pointed out that the small numbers involved (120 women in the entire project) and the voluntary character of the sample (after random selection, participation was not required) limit the reliability and the generalizability of the findings.

Women in engineering
Another program at Purdue, in its Engineering Department, was designed to meet the special needs of freshmen engineering women, particularly to address their lack of 'hands-on', technical experience compared with males' childhood experience gained through hobbies and educational experiences. The course combined laboratory experiences (with hand tools, power tools, engines, plumbing and metal) and lectures from a variety of male and female role models. Students were randomly selected from those who had expressed interest, yielding one section that was predominantly female (85 per cent) and one section that was balanced. Pre- and post-test comparisons showed that male and female participants in the special course gained in technical knowledge and self-confidence when compared with the control groups. The progress of the women in the two sections was similar, so that the gap between the experimental women and men was substantially narrowed during the one semester course (Heckert, *et al.*, 1978).

Re-entry programs for women in science
Surveys have shown that as many as 40 per cent of all women scientists drop out of the labor force at some time (Burks and Connolly, 1977). To reclaim this under-utilized segment of the labor force, re-entry programs have been developed to bring these women back into the sciences, updating their competency so that they can be full participants. A successful group of re-entry programs was funded by the Women in Science Program of the National

Science Foundation (NSF), all of which emphasized a strong academic component, although they included confidence building, study skills, and other non-academic components. [. . .] One of the most successful of these programmes is that at the University of Dayton; it provides a mechanism for career change from science to chemical and electrical engineering. [. . .] With an initial group of 71 students, 60 per cent were unemployed or underemployed, and of the 63 students who completed the programme, 61 are employed and one is in graduate school. The students received an average of three job offers each (Shaw and Bulkin, 1981).

Special classes to address problems faced by women

A thin line separates the courses described above which were explicitly designed to attract women, and in some cases were restricted to female enrolment, and the courses that will be described in this section, which were designed to address the issues in mathematics and science instruction that have been identified as particularly important for women. [. . .]

In the mid 1970s, a number of people became aware that existing mathematics curricula did not meet the needs of students who were unprepared to take calculus. When women undergraduates in particular sought fields of study and work that required quantitative skills, they found that there were no appropriate courses to address their lack of confidence and/or competence in mathematics. There were a number of factors in these students' elementary and secondary education that were identified as probable causes of this situation, clustering around the idea that mathematics is often taught in such a way that it creates strong negative feelings which are increasingly hard to overcome. Two major approaches have been used in higher education settings to assist students who lack confidence in their mathematical ability and skills – attempts to decrease math anxiety and attempts to teach mathematics in an environment that will increase confidence. [. . .]

Math anxiety

The 'math anxiety' approach was popularized by Sheila Tobias (1978), who coined the phrase that captured the frustration and difficulty faced by many students when confronted with failure in mathematics. Working with professional psychologists and mathematicians, she set up the Math Anxiety Clinic at Wesleyan University; the clinic provided counseling for students to assist them in overcoming negative feelings about themselves as learners of mathematics. The success of the clinic in enabling students to conquer their math anxiety so that they could take courses and graduate school entrance examinations that had been precluded before, led to considerable replication of this approach. Tobias (1980) has catalogued the programs and resources regarding math anxiety. [. . .]

Math without fear
An alternative approach to conquering math anxiety, has been to change the classroom environment in which mathematics is taught so as to reduce the feelings of anxiety that some students have reported feeling in traditional classes. One example of this approach is the 'Math without Fear' course established at San Francisco State University in 1975 (Resek and Rupley, 1980). Resek's premise is that a great deal of the discomfort that many students experience in mathematics courses comes from the strategy they have used to learn mathematics. Having tried to memorize a set of rules or procedures for solving problems rather than understanding mathematical concepts, they have no fallback strategy when their memories fail them. The course tries to convert these 'rule-oriented' students to a conceptual approach to mathematics that will enable them to solve problems for which they have no set algorithm to follow (Davis and Stage, 1980). Techniques used to improve students' problems solving include guessing, using physical materials to build abstract concepts, using visual representations to solve problems, small group and recreational activities, and explicit recognition of difficulties. The 'Math without Fear' course has been successful in moving 70 to 80 per cent of its students to a conceptual approach in one semester (Resek and Rupley, 1980). [. . .]

A sister course to the one at San Francisco State was started by Ruth Afflack at California State University, Long Beach. It was more formally evaluated by external evaluators (Davis and Stage, 1980), who found that students' attitudes towards mathematics and problem solving were improved, that their mathematics skills improved, and that their performance in subsequent mathematics courses exceeded their performance in courses they had attempted prior to taking 'Math without Fear'. [. . .]

Curricula designed to address special needs of women

A thin line also separates the special courses described above from the curriculum development efforts that have tried to increase females' achievement and interest in mathematics and science. As with the courses, some curricula have focused on a particular issue, such as the usefulness of mathematics for future careers, while others have taken a more global approach and have tried to influence many areas. [. . .]

Solving problems of access to careers in engineering and science (SPACES)
The SPACES project at the Lawrence Hall of Science took a broad mandate, to develop a set of 30 enrichment activities for grades three to ten that would provide career awareness and certain mathematical skills which are important for problem solving. The career awareness activities emphasize the variety of employment options available to people with good mathematics background, including non-traditional areas for women such as construction and the trades, in addition to the sciences and engineering. The mathematical skills that are

emphasized are problem solving, particularly the gathering and organizing of data, and spatial visualization.

Trial versions of the activities were used in 100 classrooms in 1980–1 and were evaluated by pre- and post-testing students on six major objectives. Significant improvement was found, above the improvement observed in the comparison group, in five of the six areas tested. While attitudes towards mathematics did not change, the SPACES students improved in career awareness (career interest, career knowledge and identification of tools) and in mathematical skills (word problem solving and spatial visualization) [. . .] (Fraser, 1982).

Career-oriented modules to explore topics in science (COMETS)
The COMETS project at the University of Kansas is a parallel in science to SPACES in math, but it has focused on the particular strategy of using role models to encourage science career interest. Each of the 24 modules described science activities that role models, called community resource people, can use to arouse interest in a science concept that is being studied by the students and is used in the person's career. Following an introductory activity, such as conducting a perc test with a geologist, the geologist can go on to describe his/her own testing of soils for various characteristics. The resource person is then asked to talk about the career and how she or he prepared for it and how it relates with other parts of her or his life, such as family roles. The materials are produced so that the introductory activities can be conducted by the classroom teacher in preparation for the resource person's visit; they provide teachers with additional information about women's contributions to science, including biographical and language arts materials [. . .] (Smith *et al.*, 1982).

Multiplying options and subtracting bias
This set of video-tapes focuses on the decision to take elective mathematics courses by addressing issues and concerns of four specific groups: junior and senior high school students, mathematics and science teachers, parents, and counselors. The program aims to increase knowledge about sex-related differences in mathematics and to improve attitudes toward females as learners of mathematics held by females, their male peers, and the adults who influence them. The tapes provide specific information about the amount of mathematics required for various careers and discuss stereotyping and differential treatment of males and females with regard to mathematics and counseling. A facilitator's guide accompanies the tapes to provide an outline for each workshop, including information and points for discussion to be held in conjunction with viewing the tapes. It is recommended by the authors (Fennema *et al.*, 1980) that the tapes be used in a full intervention – that is, with each of the target groups in a school – since the attitudes of young women are influenced by these other groups and, in some cases, are less in need of intervention than those of significant others.

An evaluation of the videotapes alone (that is, without the workshops) in nine high schools in Minnesota and Wisconsin (Fennema *et al.*, 1981), using a pre- and post-test, control group design, found that the tapes were more successful with students than with adults. Although males' increase in plans to take mathematics in high school was not as great as females' increase, males and females in the experimental group made similar gains in plans to take mathematics after high school and in their knowledge of sex-related differences in mathematics. Few changes were observed in teachers and counselors. [. . .]

Teacher education programs

As indicated above, the attitudes and knowledge of teachers are important influences on students' attitudes and achievement, and several programs have been developed to address the particular issues of concern in mathematics. [. . .]

Teacher education and mathematics (TEAM)
The TEAM program was designed to help prospective teachers at Queens College develop positive attitudes toward and deal effectively with mathematics (Chapline *et al.*, 1980). Four mathematics content modules and four attitudinal modules constitute a course to be taken prior to the math methods course, or can be used as supplementary materials in other pre-service courses. Although based on small samples, comparison of post-course measures of attitudes, math anxiety, and mathematical concepts indicated that TEAM students benefited from the program. In addition, they were able to suggest ways to counteract sex role bias in mathematics education, and more of them volunteered to teach mathematics than did a comparison group of student teachers.

Improving teachers' ability to visualize mathematics
A course was developed at the University of Washington that had three goals: to improve elementary teachers' spatial skills, problem solving skills, and attitudes towards mathematics. The 30-hour course focused on three aspects of spatial ability: visual imagery, mental rotation, and mental transformation. [. . .] the tasks proceeded from those requiring no movement of the image, to movement of the complete image, to movement of different parts of the image; from two dimensions to three dimensions; and from concrete representations to pictures. The instructional strategies moved from free exploration to structured analysis. All work was done in pairs, and students were encouraged to discuss their ideas so that they would become aware of their own thinking and of individual differences in frames of reference. Significant improvement was found in three classes of teachers on three spatial tests, a college level algebra word problem-solving test, and five attitude scales (Cook and Kersh, 1980).

EQUALS
The EQUALS program is an inservice program for teachers, administrators and counselors, grades K–12, to assist educators in using materials and activities to promote the participation and achievement of women and minorities in

mathematics. Educators attend 10 or 30-hour inservice workshops during the school year. They collect and analyze research findings on sex differences in mathematics participation and career aspirations, explore math-related fields of work and study, participate in activities that promote improved student attitudes and understanding of mathematics, develop problem solving skills, and plan inservice presentations to disseminate EQUALS to other educators.

The evaluation of the EQUALS program has examined its impact on several levels. The most directly affected participants, the educators who attend the workshops, keep journals and report their activities at the subsequent workshops. Nearly all of the activities and teaching strategies are used by a majority of the teachers, with an average implementation level for each activity of over 70 per cent. A follow-up survey conducted in 1981 of all participants since 1977 found that the majority were still using EQUALS material.

The effect of the materials on students has been investigated by a pre- and post-test, control group design using a career awareness survey and a mathematics attitude scale for older students and pictures of bears in various occupations for younger students. Over the years of evaluation the results have varied, but have indicated modest improvement in attitudes towards mathematics and increased interest in math-related fields. An additional measure of effectiveness has been student enrolment in elective mathematics classes. While there are many factors influencing student enrolment, including availability of qualified teachers and changes in state requirements, there are indications that increased participation of girls has been associated with EQUALS activity by teachers in some schools (Kreinberg, 1981). [. . .] A handbook has been produced by the program (Kasebergm *et al.*, 1980) that has allowed others to conduct EQUALS workshops without direct assistance from the program. [. . .]

Extra curricular activities for women

The preceding sections have described a variety of programs that have attempted to change the educational experiences of girls and women in educational institutions, either by developing special classes or curricula, or by changing the outlook or behavior of teachers and counselors. A complementary approach to these interventions has been in the development of a variety of extra curricular activities. [. . .]

The visiting women scientists program
The idea of inviting a woman scientist or mathematician to speak to a group of secondary students about her career has been tried by a variety of groups. [. . .] In 1977, a large scale demonstration program was contracted by NSF to the Research Triangle Institute, to design and implement a pilot Visiting Women Scientists program, the purpose of which was to motivate female high school students to consider careers in science, including engineering, mathematics, the social sciences, and the biological and physical science.

The program included visits by 40 women scientists to 110 high schools across the United States. Approximately 40 per cent of a national sample of high schools accepted the offer to participate in the pilot program, and they were randomly assigned to experimental and control groups. The visit of the woman scientist to the participating high schools included some combination of the following: large and small group meetings with female students, sessions with individual co-educational classes, and meetings with school staff members. Scientists talked about their jobs, their educational and personal backgrounds, and ways of resolving problems associated with combining a career in science with a full family life.

A major goal of the program was to encourage high school girls to seek more information about scientific careers (Weiss *et al.*, 1978). Students in both experimental and control schools were given postcards for requesting further information, and the return rate from experimental schools was significantly greater than from control schools (21 vs. 6 per cent). A survey of school staff with career guidance responsibility found that 57 per cent of the experimental schools versus 38 per cent of the control schools reported that more than the usual number of female students had sought information about scientific careers. [. . .]

Expanding your horizons in science and mathematics conference
Beginning with two conferences in the San Francisco Bay area in 1976, there were 43 'Expanding Your Horizons' conferences sponsored by the Math/Science Network in 1982 [. . .] The Math/Science Network is a group of over 1,000 scientists, educators and community people who work together to increase girls' and women's participation in math-related and non-traditional fields, and their sponsorship of these conferences is one of their most extensive efforts. The purposes of the conferences, which are held in the Spring on college campuses, are to increase students' interest in science and mathematics, to foster awareness of career opportunities in math and science-related fields, and to provide students with an opportunity to meet and form personal contacts with women working in traditionally male fields.

While individual conference committees plan and conduct their own programs, the Network provides guidance and technical assistance (Koltnow, 1979). Features common to the conferences are panel presentations, 'hands-on' workshops, and career workshops with women in non-traditional, math and science-related fields. Evaluation includes surveys on the day of the conference and follow-up surveys six to nine months after the conference. Students have increased the number of math, science and computer classes they plan to take in high school and have learned more about these career fields. Six months after the conference, they actually enrolled in as many or more mathematics courses as they had indicated that they planned at the conclusion of the conference, and they had taken a number of other actions to further their knowledge of and experience related to these careers. A report on the longitudinal study and a kit for evaluating interventions like this are available from the Math/Science

Resource Center, Mills, College, Oakland, CA 94613 (Sheila Humphreys, Principal Investigaror). [. . .]

Rutgers' science career workshop
Freshman and sophomore women from colleges in New Jersey attended a one-day workshop where 12 scientists spoke about their work and personal backgrounds and then led informal discussions for each of the science disciplines represented. The students who attended the workshop filled out a questionnaire six months later, in which they reported that the workshop stimulated their thinking (90 per cent), that they had learned useful information about job requirements and salaries (85 per cent), and that it was possible to combine a science career with a family (75 per cent) (Cohen and Elgart, 1981). The following proportions of career-related actions were taken by the participants and attributed to the workshop: enrolled in a science course (96 per cent took action, 14 per cent of whom attributed it to the workshop); engaged in research (24 per cent, 44 per cent); joined science-related organization (29 per cent, 30 per cent); sought contacts with women scientists (29 per cent, 60 per cent); sought information in books or magazines (71 per cent, 67 per cent); sent for science-career pamphlets (26 per cent, 62 per cent); and watched scientific television program (79 per cent, 28 per cent). The discrimination in their attributions to the workshop – low for actions they were likely to pursue such as coursework; high for actions they learned about at the workshop, such as the willingness of female scientists to speak with them about their careers – gives confidence that the workshop probably did bring about some additional career-related activity on the part of the students. [. . .]

Summary and conclusions

The programs reviewed in this chapter share several elements that provide guidance for future efforts to increase women's participation and achievement in mathematics, science and engineering. Three general features are present in nearly all of the successful programs: strong academic emphases, multiple strategies, and systems approaches.

Strong academic emphasis
The causes and mechanisms of the sex-related differences in science and mathematics achievement are not clearly understood, but program planners have acknowledged their existence by designing curricula that address the specific skills identified by research as potential causes. Thus, tools for developing spatial ability, problem solving ability and mechanical sophistication are present in many programs. A commitment to extending competence by enrolling in advanced courses and acquiring marketable skills is presented as an essential goal for young women in science. By defining such specific and

measurable goals, the programs can evaluate their efforts and demonstrate measurable gains to others. The presence of evaluation and the link to research strengthens both program development and dissemination.

Multiple strategies

Most successful programs have made use of more than one strategy for increasing women's participation in science. They have tried to influence the environment in which mathematics and science are taught – to make these fields accessible to women and to present them as viable options for women. Role models of women in math and science-related fields are highly motivational for students because they also deliver information and strategies for achieving in science activities. Hands-on experiences, particularly in all-female groups, promote confidence as well as skills that can be relied on in subsequent courses. Combined goals of confidence and competence enhance each other, as do the complementary attitudes of enjoying and appreciating the usefulness of quantitative activities. Given the complex origins of the low participation of women in science, it makes sense that multiple strategies are needed to solve the problem; in practice, it is not only sensible, but effective to use several strategies.

Systems approach

[. . .] The problems for women in science are not theirs alone. The expectations and sex-stereotyped practices of parents and teachers, their lack of awareness of the importance of mathematics and science proficiency for all students, and their lack of experience in problem solving and spatial skills, which they fail to develop in females, all contribute to women's difficulties. Some of the programs described above, notably 'Multiplying Options and Subtracting Bias', have developed materials for several target groups, and others are extending their efforts to include parents, administrators, teachers, and students.

Final thought

These elements – strong academic emphasis, multiple strategies and systems approaches – represent the strengths of programs for increasing women's participation and achievement in math, science and engineering, but they also represent sound educational practice. One might argue that girls and women are more susceptible than are boys and men to poor educational practices such as learning mathematics as a collection of rules or science as a set of formulae. But as long as so few women reach their potential in the sciences, specific strategies that address the reasons for their low participation and achievement must be designed, implemented and evaluated.

References

Aldrich, M.L. (1982). *Women and Mathematics: Recent Programs*. Paper presented at the American Education Research Association, New York.

Aldrich, M.L. and Hall, P.W. (1980). *Programs in Science, Mathematics, and Engineering for Women and Girls in the United States (1976–1978)*. American Association for the Advancement of Science.

Brody, L. and Fox, L.H. (1980). 'An accelerative intervention program for mathematically gifted girls'. In Fox, L.H., Brody, L. and Tobin, D. (eds), *Women and the Mathematical Mystique*. Johns Hopkins University Press.

Brown, L.H. (1976). *The Retention of Women in the Science Disciplines* (Final Report 1973–1975, Fund for Improvement of Post Secondary Education). Purdue University.

Burks, E.L. and Connolly, T. (1977). 'Women in science and engineering: characteristics and experiences of established professionals', *Engineering Education*. December pp. 234–40.

Chapline, R., Newman, C., Denker, E. and Tittle, C.K. (1980). *Final Report: Teacher Education and Mathematics Project*. Queens College, City University of New York.

Cohen, C.E. and Elgart, C.K. (1981). *Promoting the Entry of Women Into Science Careers: Report on a Career Workshop for College Women*. Unpublished manuscript, Douglass College. New Brunswick, NJ, Rutgers University.

Cook, N. and Kersh, M.E. (1980). 'Improving teachers' ability to visualize mathematics'. In Karplus, R. (ed.), *Proceedings of the Fourth International Conference for the Psychology of Mathematics Education*. Berkeley, Lawrence Hall of Science.

Cooperative Institutional Research Program (1974–82). *The American Freshman: National Norms for Fall 1971–1980*. Los Angeles, UCLA, Graduate School of Education.

Davis, B.G. and Stage, E.K. (1980). *Evaluation Report for a Math Learning Center with Microcomputers*. Berkeley, University of California.

Downie, D., Slesnick, T. and Stenmark, J.K. (1981). *Math for Girls and Other Problem Solvers*. Berkeley, University of California.

Ernest, J. (1976). *Mathematics and Sex*. Santa Barbara, University of California.

Fennema, E., Becker, A.D., Wolleat, P.L. and Pedro, J.D. (1980). *Multiplying Options and Subtracting Bias*. Reston, National Council of Teachers of Mathematics.

Fennema, E., Wolleat, P.L., Pedro, J.D. and Becker, A.D. (1981). 'Increasing women's participation in mathematics: an intervention study', *Journal for Research in Mathematics Education*, Vol. 12, pp. 3–14.

Fox, L.H. (1976). 'Sex differences in mathematical precocity: bridging the gap'. In Keating, D.P. (ed.), *Intellectual Talent: Research and Development*. Johns Hopkins University Press.

Fraser, S. (1982). *SPACES: Solving Problems of Access to Careers in Engineering and Science*. Berkeley, University of California.

Heckert, B.L., LeBold, W.K., Butler, B., Knigga, M., Smith, C.D., Blalock, M. and Hoover, E. (1978). *A Model Research Program to Provide Equity for Women Entering Engineering*. Paper presented at the American Educational Research Association, Toronto, Canada.

Kaseberg, A., Kreinberg, N. and Downie, D. (1980). *Use EQUALS to promote the participaion of women in mathematics*. Berkeley, University of California.

Koltnow, J. (1979). *Expanding Your Horizons: Conferences for Young Women Interested in New Career Options*. Washington, DC, U.S. Department of Education.

Kreinberg, N. (1981). '1000 teachers later: women, mathematics and the components of change', *Public Affairs Report*, Vol. 22, pp. 1–7.

MacDonald, C.T. (1980). 'An experiment in mathematics education at the college level'. In Fox, L.H., Brody, L., and Tobin, D. (eds), *Women and the Mathematical Mystique*. Johns Hopkins University Press.

National Research Council (1980). *Science, Engineering and Humanities Doctorates in the United States: 1979 Profile*. National Academy of Sciences.

Resek, D. and Rupley, W.H. (1980). 'Combatting "mathophobia" with a conceptual approach to mathematics', *Educational Studies in Mathematics*, Vol. 11, pp. 423–41.

Sells, L. (1975). *Sex, Ethnic, and Field Differences in Doctoral Outcomes*. PhD Dissertation. Berkeley, University of California.

Shaw, C.M. and Bulkin, B.J. (1981). *Reentry Programs: Their Design and Impact*. Unpublished manuscript, University of Dayton.

Smith, W.S., Molitor, L.L., Nelson, B.J. and Matthew, C.E. (1982). *Career Oriented Modules to Explore Topics in Science*. Lawrence, University of Kansas.

Tobias, S. (1978). *Overcoming Math Anxiety*. W.W. Norton.

Tobias, S. (1980). *Paths to Programs for Intervention: Math Anxiety, Math Avoidance, and Reentry Mathematics*. Washington DC, Institute for the Study of Anxiety in Learning.

Vetter, B. (1981). 'Women in science and engineering: trends in participation', *Science*, Vol. 214, pp. 1313–21.

Weiss, I., Pace, C. and Conaway, L.E. (1978). *The visiting women scientists pilot program 1978: Highlights Report*, North Carolina, Research Triangle Institute.

Name Index

Subject Index